COUPLE COMMUNICATION FOR RELATIONSHIP GROWTH

A ROADMAP TO DEEPER CONNECTION

GRANT MORGAN

INTRODUCTION

In the intricate and ever-evolving dance of relationships, communication stands as both the cornerstone and the bridge between partners. This book is crafted to illuminate the path toward deeper connection, offering couples a compass to navigate the myriad challenges and joys of communication. Whether it's the subtle art of expressing needs without blame or the delicate task of holding space for vulnerability, this guide delves into the nuances that make up meaningful exchanges.

Couples today face a unique set of challenges, from digital misunderstandings to the complexities of diverse relationship structures. Recognizing this, the book celebrates the rich tapestry of relationships, embracing diversity in all its forms, be it cultural, LGBTQ+, or nontraditional. It acknowledges that each couple's journey is distinct, with its own set of dynamics and rhythms.

Readers are invited to explore the common hurdles that impede communication, such as feeling unheard or misunderstood, and the frustration of one-sided efforts. The text validates these experiences while offering practical, actionable strategies to overcome them. Through real-life scripts, exercises, and reflection prompts, couples are equipped to transform theoretical insights into tangible progress.

What sets this book apart is its commitment to inclusivity and practicality. It offers a wealth of tools, from step-by-step exercises and digital communication strategies to customizable worksheets and diverse scenarios that resonate with real-world experiences. By fostering an environment of mutual responsibility and shared growth, the book encourages both partners to participate actively in the journey toward a more profound connection.

Ultimately, this book is an invitation to couples to invest in their relationship and see communication as a dynamic skill that can be honed and deepened. It promises not just a roadmap but a supportive companion for those committed to nurturing their relationship and creating a lasting, fulfilling connection.

Table of Contents

GRANT MORGAN

COUPLE COMMUNICATION FOR RELATIONSHIP GROWTH

CHAPTER 1

BUILDING A SAFE SPACE FOR DIALOGUE

DEFINING EMOTIONAL SAFETY

When it comes to intimate relationships, emotional safety should be discussed as one of the most crucial factors in the establishment of a real connection and advancement. Emotional safety is a situation in which both people are confident enough to share their innermost emotions, thoughts, and fears without risk of disapproval or rejection. It is the fabric that knits the line of a relationship so that all people involved in it feel valued, understood, and respected.

This factor of emotional safety consists of making a setting in which both people may express themselves freely. This allows not only listening to what one another says but also having the ability to hear and comprehend the feelings behind the words. It involves the determination of nurturing an environment in which both spouses are free to be themselves without the fear of being mocked, ignored in general, or misinterpreted. Such comfort makes a person reduce their guard and connect on a deeper and more meaningful level.

Emotional safety is not an achievement that can be attained once, but it is an ongoing process that needs to be tweaked and exercised. It entails consistent usage of empathy where spouses work hard to understand situations from the perspective of the other person. Such understanding among each other plays a very critical role in avoiding misunderstanding and rectifying a conflict in a friendly way. Empathy entails recognizing and accepting what the other feels, even when he or she does not agree with the other person, since he or she may not have the sense of what the other is feeling.

Trust is key in the creation of emotional safety. It is developed by performing the same actions that will show reliability, honesty, and support. Trust can be strengthened when partners follow the agreements, confidentiality, and show up for each other. Over time, this practice stores a pool of positive incidents that strengthens the feeling that both partners are committed to each other.

Nonverbal communication is yet another component of emotional safety. Contact with a patient may be verbal as well as non-verbal, including eye contact, a welcoming smile, or even a touch, giving encouragement and support. Such nuances can contribute to strengthening the oral assurances and make it a more complete feeling of security and affiliation.

A healthy relationship also allows for the sharing of ideas regarding boundaries and needs. The partners ought to share their desires freely, explaining what makes them feel safe and respected in the relationship. It may involve establishing limits about some subjects, coming to terms with how conflicting situations should be resolved, or creating a judgment-free zone where everyone is free to speak whatever is on their mind without the fear of judgment.

Moreover, emotional safety means bravery in being naked. It is about the risk of opening yourself to one another with fears, dreams, insecurities, and being sure that such disclosures will be received with understanding and encouragement. Such weakness leads to an even more intimate relationship as the other party learns and comprehends deeply the internal world of another person, learning to value it.

After all, emotional stability is an issue when building a relationship that gives both sides of the relationship space to expand and develop. It is a mutual responsibility to raise a relationship that is strong, flexible, and based on respect and understanding. Emotional safety should be prioritized in a relationship so that partners can create a strong bond of everlasting affection and togetherness.

CREATING A SAFE SPACE CONTRACT

When it comes to building relationships, the key factor in this field is the creation of a setting that will help both parties involved feel they are emotionally safe. This space is commonly known as a safe space, and it goes beyond a physical place; it is a mental refuge where couples are free to think and share their emotions, fearing neither disdain nor vengeance. An effective partnership and zone of possibility take purposefulness and recognition to build them and establish a foundation.

A safe space in a relationship is all about not being afraid to be vulnerable. It is an obligation to listen emphatically and be kind, even in the event that disagreements arise. This area is enhanced by respecting each other and the guarantee that the two partners are devoted to each other's emotional well-being. Creating such an environment is a tangible process that may be formalized in the form of a so-called safe space contract. This is not a legal contract but a unanimous understanding that states the guidelines and practices that should be followed by the two partners so as to ensure a favorable environment of care and understanding.

The first step in establishing a safe space contract is to determine the meaning of safety to each of the partners. This includes glaring conversations of personal boundaries, emotional hot buttons, and particular needs that each one of us has that make him or her feel safe. The partners are not only favored to share their former experiences in which they felt safe or unsafe, they also use them as a learning instrument so as to make the terms of the contract. This is to have a common place on what emotional safety would be like and to form an agreement on action that could enhance it.

Making the space safe is also part of it, and entails establishing what can be called safe words or signs, which can be relied upon during the discussions when one partner experiences overload or a need to take a break. These cues are most important in challenging conversations, as the partners can de-escalate the situation without having the sensation of leaving the discussion behind. Another factor leading to the establishment of a calm and centered mindset prior to addressing potentially sensitive topics is establishing a pre-conversation ritual where both parties agree to engage in a deep-breathing exercise or a moment of silence in order to establish a certain level of calm and centeredness before addressing the even more sensitive topics.

The context under which the conversations are held is very important as well. To ensure concentration and show a respectful attitude to the conversation, it is better to identify a distraction-free place that is also free of any digital distractions. The value of the discussion is that it would make both parties feel that they are fully noticed and that what they talk about is both vital and safe.

The establishment of a safe space is not a one-time exercise. It mandates frequent check-ins on safety to determine how well the two are adhering to the agreement and make corrections when necessary. The check-ins also give a chance to brag about the accomplishments and clear up any situation where there was a missed moment when the safe space became damaged, making sure that both partners stay curious and faithful to the contract.

The establishment of a safe space contract is essentially a process that involves two or more sides building a stronger base for the relationship. It entails the shared interest in the personal development and joy of each other, resulting in a partnership that will support, embrace, and feel that the other is appreciated and understood. This proactive way of communicating and developing emotional security not only strengthens the relationship between the partners but also enables one to endure even in the hard moments, making the relationship healthy.

ENVIRONMENT AND CONTEXT

In all relationships, the setting and the surroundings help to influence the nature of the relationship's communication processes. The context under which conversations can have a great impact on the way partners communicate and do not misinterpret the notions. Knowing this aspect of a communication process, we understand that it is not only the words that are said, but also the type of atmosphere and environment in which these words are said.

Think about two partners who want to talk about a sensitive matter in a crowded cafe where the dishes and noise of the chatter of other people are all around. There may be interference and no privacy, attracting some obstructions to their capacity to engage and listen. Conversely, a serene, relaxing environment at home, maybe having soft lights and a lack of distractions, can provide an atmosphere of open and truthful discussion. With the help of such an environment, they will be more open to each other and feel safe and liberal.

The situation also involves the emotional and psychological condition of each partner when communicating. When a partner has had a stressful day, workwise, he or she may not be in a good position to hold a meaningful conversation. Seeing and accepting these personal backgrounds can aid the partners in taking each dialogue in a more empathetic way, with a greater degree of patience, guided by an ability to communicate more efficiently.

In addition, past events between two people affect the present communications. Negative and positive experiences that partners have in the past may tint the way one partner will interpret the words and actions of the other. A partner who had previously felt that their voice was not heard might enter a conversation defensively or warily because he or she expects to be disregarded once more. On the other hand, a track record of communicating in helpful and affirming ways can create goodwill on a sort of open account and allow the process of getting through a crisis to be smoother.

Location also depends on culture and society. Having a different culture can come with divergent expectations and conventions associated with communication. An example can be given, whereby, in a certain culture, directness and assertiveness can be valued, whereas in another culture, harmony and indirect communication can be prioritized. These differences can be understood and respected to ensure that partners close the gap and get to know each other better.

The communication context, in the digital era, has been enlarged to encompass virtual spaces. Messages, emailing, and video conferencing constitute a major aspect of the interactions of couples. These media have their problems and advantages as well. On the one hand, they can be convenient, quick in nature, and enable people to meet globally without consideration of distance or proximity; on the other hand, the absence of non-verbal cues can result in misunderstandings. Digital communication, therefore, requires one to be conscious of one's tone and be clear in one's messages as a way of preserving a healthy relationship.

In the end, the context (environment) is not a given; it is plastic and is amenable to deliberate interventions. To foster healthy communication, couples can also create conditions conducive to positive communication by paying attention to the space in which they talk about important issues and developing rituals to enhance bonding and knowledge. These can be done by taking time to meet regularly in a calm environment or making boundaries on digital turf so as to avoid distractions, which would increase the level of communication.

In brief, the interaction between environment and context in relation to couple communication acquires depth. Being conscious and mindful to handle these factors actively, partners can develop a solid base that fosters growth, comprehension, and fitness of their relationship. The awareness not only intensifies the current discussion but also enhances the overall relationship, setting the milieu for an even more profound and rewarding relationship.

ONGOING SAFETY CHECK-INS

The safety check-in is another important concept in couple communication because it minimizes the risk of being hurt or cultivating wounds. Such check-in is not just a formality; these rituals serve to ensure that the couple will have an open line of communication and will make both members feel that their voice and emotions are heard, appreciated, and felt safe to communicate.

The crux of performing regular safety check-ins is the fact that they provide a routine avenue for partners to express their issues, their happiness, and what they require without judgment or retaliation. Such sessions are not set aside only to solve conflicts but are part of the daily upkeep of the relationship. Through such frequent communication, couples can solve small problems before they degenerate into big ones, thus improving the peace in the relationship.

One of the important things about these check-ins is that a protective and comfortable environment is developed. This would require localizing a special time and place where possible distractions are avoided and partners can give undivided attention to one another—schedule visits with your spouse regularly, whether weekly. Even dinner talks, as a monthly meet-up with a spouse, are a way of reinforcing the value of such meetings and the willingness of both spouses to engage and be frank.

In these check-ins, each of the two individuals must consider the conversation not as a criticism but as an opportunity to be curious. This includes posing some open questions and actually listening to the answers with an aim to listen, not to counter. In this way, partners are able to touch into deeper feelings and problems which may not come out directly. Due to this approach, the previously unaddressed potential negative effect on the relationship is managed by discussing how disagreeing partners felt during the encounter and what could be changed in the future, where their communication received more consideration.

In addition, these check-ins remind the couple that they are mutually involved in ensuring the health of the relationship. They help fix an eye and tell someone how very much your hard work is appreciated, how grateful you are for the big and little things that many times go unnoticed in the rush and noise of everyday life. This recognition has the potential to make a big impact on the emotional bank account of the relationship, causing a greater feeling of connection and appreciation.

Moreover, regular safety checks may be structured according to the peculiarities of a given relationship. It is recommended that couples establish their rituals and routines to instill in them their personalities and the couple's objectives. It is preferable to do so either via a rather structured agenda or a more casual one-on-one dialogue. Still, the important thing is to locate whatever works best and feels natural to both partners. Such customization not only enhances the enjoyment of the check-ins but also endows them with greater meaning since they stand out as a representation of a couple in question and their relationship.

To recap it all, one of the most significant parts of couple communication is safety check-ins. They have a good framework, which is at the same time not constraining, and thus it allows partners to stay in their relationships and face the complexities of the same with empathy and understanding. By focusing on these routine conversations, the couples that comprise them have the opportunity to establish a strong union that can survive the challenges that are bound to come their way, all this as they increase their level of emotional connection and respect for each other.

CHAPTER 2

Understanding Emotional Needs

IDENTIFYING PERSONAL NEEDS

Knowing what one needs on their part is central to the creation of a balanced relationship. Every person has their baggage, which will be their emotional, psychological, and even physical needs, and once identified and treated, can easily help build mutual understanding and closeness in a relationship.

The process of searching for these needs starts with self-analysis. Couples should be advised to go deep inside themselves, to think about what really makes them happy and what they do not have. This sense of self will form the base of open and honest communication where both partners are able to express their needs without any fear of judgment or rejection.

In some cases, one might not know how to express his/her needs or rather address them because such an individual has been socialized in a way that masks or removes the desire to express needs or rather disregards it according to the societal conditioning or rather relationship patterns which the individual has experienced. These barriers must be brought down through the construction of an environment that fosters and encourages the principle of vulnerability.

This process encompasses listening, which is vital in the process. Active listening is not merely hearing words; it encompasses a sympathetic interplay in which one of the partners is really interested in listening to what the other partner has to say, and that he/she is trying to see the other person from his/her point of view also. This deep aspect of listening aids in the confirmation of feelings and needs of each of the partners and eventually promotes the sense of being understood and cherished.

Practically, what couples can do is to initiate some time they can use to address their needs. This may be in the form of a checking arrangement where one checks in every week, where each partner has the liberty to express freely their current emotional status, what is lacking, and what they need to feel more connected and satisfied in the relationship. These conversations are to be done without blame and in a curious manner, with the aim of deciphering and not repairing.

It is also empowering when the partners investigate and construct the needs in various means of communication, either linguistic or non-linguistic, written, or even creatively through the arts or music. This communication diversity can assist in evoking very complex feelings that, in some situations, cannot be explained with a single word.

Validations of personal needs are not a process but a continuous conversation. Due to the changes in life situations, needs might change as well. The constant reflection and communication make both partners understand each other's changing yearnings for each other, enabling them to come up with adaptations and accommodations that eventually strengthen the bond.

Furthermore, the desire to express one's needs is not a weakness or selfishness. Instead, it is the essential element of a sound relationship. By knowing what the other partner needs and helping to provide the need, a strong and resilient relationship is formed, where both partners have mutual respect and understanding.

Finally, determining personal needs is an issue of establishing the connection when both counterparts feel visual, audible, and loved. It is concerned with forging an alliance that now focuses on individual development and, in the meantime, cultivates joint work to grow the relationship. With the adoption of the practice, the couples are in a position to build a culture that not only satisfies but also glorifies the desires that bring long-lasting intimacy and trust.

Expressing Needs Clearly

It seems that in the dance of relationships, perhaps the most important thing for partners to develop is the art of being able to communicate effectively and tactfully about what they need. It is not just an ability to convey what one wants but a more sophisticated way of knowing how to put such desire in a way that will not result in confrontation.

The core of needs expression, therefore, is the understanding that needs are not requirements or evidence of weaknesses. They are rather the primary aspects that support the relationship between the two partners so that they can feel appreciated and comprehended. Acknowledging this changes the psyche to an otherwise potentially challenging airing of needs to a chance of further intimacy and one another's growth.

Self-awareness is a very important precursor to this process. There is a need to practice introspection in the partners to be able to come up with their individual needs, so that they can then communicate with each other. This includes thinking of what is actually important to them, what can make them feel loved, secure, and supported. One example is how one might understand that after an argument or a scheduled follow-up, they require reassurance in order to feel bonded with the other person.

When these needs are established, they then have to be spelled out in a very concrete but non-incriminating manner. This is a way of making use of the I statement, which concentrates on oneself instead of accusing the partner. Using the examples, instead of saying that someone never lets them know about his plans, more constructively, they can say something like: I feel appreciated when we go over our plans together. Such language not only conveys the necessity but also encourages the partner to exchange a dialogue, but not a response.

The timing and setting should also be considered when expressing needs. The selection of a time when the partners are on neutral ground, so to speak, can do a lot of good for the communication efforts. Moreover, it is important to make sure that a corresponding environment is created where open communication can be realized without any distractions and pressures, as such environments could contribute significantly to the way in which the message is received.

Further, partners must be aware of cultural and personal differences between them, which can affect their communication behavior. What appears to be a direct statement of needs in a given culture may be interpreted as brutish or obnoxious to a different culture. It is crucial to be sensitive to these details and enter the discussion with an open mind to dialogue, and this can be used as a way of avoiding misunderstandings and making the discussion more inclusive.

When presenting needs, it is also good to exercise empathy. It not only refers to saying what one needs but also to being able to listen and become aware of the needs of the partner. When a partner does not feel understood and confirmed, an empathetic conversation will help both parties leave the situation feeling understood and confirmed and establish stronger and more supportive relationships.

Last but not least, needs should be viewed as the ever-in-progress process of expression. Relationships change, and therefore, the needs of people within the relationship change. Periodic review and re-definition of such needs keep both partners oriented to the needs of the other as well as to their sense of change.

As far as learning how to articulate needs, couples will be able to turn the areas that can develop strain into the points of connection and improvement. The skill is effective in promoting the well-being of an individual and strengthening the relationship, which acts as a stabilizing factor in spite of the unavoidable dangers of shared life.

SCRIPTS FOR EVERYDAY SCENARIOS

When we talk about everyday life and relationships, couples have to go through a variety of circumstances that may both strengthen their relationships or unravel them slowly. The best thing to do in such situations is, by all means, to ensure effective communication, compassion, and clarity. This second part goes into functional scripts, which are aimed at handling those situations that occur in everyday life and thus give a couple a guideline on how to communicate in such a manner that can be helpful in fostering respect and understanding.

Take the example of the morning rush, both couples are getting ready to go to work. Transactions can very quickly hijack their conversational efforts, where the point of their talk is based entirely on logistics and not connection. The plain script to change this moment might be that I find the way you handle it really well in the morning chaos. Can I help you at all today?" This is not just a word of gratitude, but it opens up space to support one another.

Shifting to the evening hours, when both members of a family come back home tired from a working day, it is essential to create some time for reconnection. Rather than barreling into chores or other single-person activities, take a moment to talk with one another, such as, How was your day, really? Makes deeper sharing more than just superficial. This script reminds the partners to stop and actively listen, which brings the feeling that they are heard and appreciated.

Another ordinary difficulty is experiencing the fine art of voicing needs without being accusative. As an example, when one partner wishes to have more quality time, one may state, I miss being together as we always were. Is it possible to have a special evening this week? This will be centered on the positive desire and not on what they lack, and thereby, it will be easier for the other partner to act positively on the same.

A go-to script can help avoid ratcheting up the conflict in the heat of the moment to find a way to come to a resolution. In the middle of a quarrel, one of the sides may calmly mention something like, "I should have some time to think this through. Could we rest and discuss this in a little while?" Not only does this script take into consideration the importance of having some space, but there is also the promise that the matter is something that one will come to again, and doing so is sufficient enough to help defuse the tension and avert a misunderstanding.

Where one of the couple has a more specific communication style, i.e., more direct as compared to the other, who is reserved, there can be scripts to mediate this difference. A partner may respond, telling you that he or she understands that the two of you have different approaches, and he or she appreciates your side of the story. Is there any way to come to meet in the middle?" This script reflects the legitimacy of the style of both partners and fosters cooperation instead of confrontation.

Humor is also a potent force when applied to day-to-day living. Witty script such as: Well, it seems like you and I are both a bit hangry, so maybe we should order it in tonight and make a ceasefire? Has the potential to make things less serious and channel the energy into a common solution.

Lastly, gratitude can be demonstrated using certain scripts that help to improve daily communications. Instead of saying a generic thank you, a more personal please can be said, such as Thank you for taking me out of the hook on dinner tonight, it made me relax better, which will be more positive.

With the help of these scripts, couples will find it much easier to go through everyday occasions and turn routine interactions into ones that will lead to a deeper connection and a better understanding of each other. These scripts are not canned scripts but flexible models couples can customize to their peculiarities so their communication can be a growth and harmony tool and not an obstacle.

BALANCING NEEDS AND BOUNDARIES

The nature of human relations is a fine dance that requires awareness and expression of what each person desires and needs, as well as balancing those requirements with those of the other. This dance needs both partners to balance themselves and see that the lives of each other and the pair are preserved. The main thing is the continuous conversation in which there is a sense of being heard, validated, and respected by both spouses.

In a relationship, we should understand that needs are the most important aspect of a relationship. Needs are not things that put a strain or are a requirement on someone; needs are requirements of a healthy connection. They involve emotional, physical, and psychological aspects that determine the feeling of satisfaction and happiness in an individual. To have a successful marriage, each individual needs to feel free of the insecurity of judgment and rejection as they share these needs with their companion.

The helpful way to express needs commences with self-recognition. Partners are always urged to take inner probing activities that enable them to define what they actually need in the relationship. This can be reassurance, quality, or being there during bad times. After these needs have been articulated, the next step is to communicate these needs. Statements that begin with I such as I feel connected when we talk together in the evenings are useful in helping one to express their needs without blaming or causing a defensive attitude.

Boundaries play an equally crucial role since they protect in all situations, as they come in the form of guidelines that safeguard the emotional and physical space of both partners. Boundaries are not about introducing distance but making both people feel safe and respected within the environment so they can fully flourish. Boundaries that work are open, clearly communicated, and reviewed at least every once in a while to adapt to shifts in the nature of the relationship.

The difference between rigid and flexible edges is necessary. Hard boundaries cannot be negotiated to protect core values and the well-being of a person. In contrast, flexible boundaries enhance the sense of ease and compromise that a situation or relationship might require. An example of a commonly used hard boundary would be, for example, no phones at dinner to make sure there is no distraction and everyone is present. The flexible boundary may instead entail taking finances up at a more amiable time, say, after the children are asleep.

General boundary checks have to be made regularly, particularly when there are changes taking place or other life transitions. Such communications give partners chances to rethink and renegotiate their boundaries so that they can be topical and capable of supporting the personal growth of the participants in the relationships as well as the development of the relationship.

Employing the needs and bound needs dynamic involves the decision to be empathetic and communicate openly. Couples need to work toward listening to one another, validating their life experiences, and reacting to others with empathy instead of defensively. This includes the strength behind showing vulnerability and the responsibility of respecting each other in front of the importance and range.

Finally, the equilibrium of needs and boundaries is a process that continues to change with the relationship. It is characterized by respecting each other, adjusting to one another, and also sharing a sense of commitment towards developing a partnership where the two parties feel appreciated and aided. With such a balanced approach, couples will be able to develop a healthy, lasting relationship that can flourish on understanding, empathy, and mutual growth.

CHAPTER 3

Active Listening Techniques

THE ANATOMY OF LISTENING

Listening is not just done by hearing the words, but it is a complex exercise that lies at the core of successful communication between people. Listening requires mind and heart, not just the perception of sound, but literally the reception of the speaker and knowing and feeling what he is trying to put across. It is more about establishing an environment where the speaker can feel important and in touch with the speaker, and building the connection beyond the conversation.

To listen means to give full attention. This involves putting other things away and giving full attention to the speaker. It has to do with the real world, with eye contact, acknowledgment nods, and body language, which conveys acceptance and welcoming of information. These non-verbal messages cannot be underestimated because they follow the message and prove that somebody is really interested in what the speaker is saying. The feeling that is generated through listening is one of respect and care, which is the essential building block of trust in any relationship.

Besides attachment, listening needs to be attended to mentally. This means the processing of the information being communicated, the emotions behind the information, and the context. It is not about being able to wait till it is your turn to talk, but to be actually interested in what the person speaking thinks. This psychological presence in the mind is expressed by the use of small encouraging words such as, I see or Mm-hmm which shows the listener is listening keenly to the conversation.

The feature that makes the difference between active and passive hearing is the way active listening influences relationships. The effect of making the partners feel heard is that it eliminates defensiveness and creates an atmosphere of safety and trust. This security is the core because it fosters open and honest communication where the partners can relate and speak out without fear of criticism or rejection. Listening to one another can help close distances, build trust, and strengthen the emotional connection between two people in a relationship.

To foster such listening, couples may undertake listening exercises that help them to practice listening. An example of such a practice is what is known as the listening switch, where you take turns to talk, and you are allowed to listen to the other partner without interrupting them. This game is useful not only for training listening but also for teaching focusing on each other and understanding each other better.

The other important element of listening includes reflection and paraphrasing. This entails rephrasing what is said by the speaker, and this further aids in clarifying the message understood and also makes sure that the message is correctly received. Such phrases as "So what I hear is..." They may be used as checks to clarify, and avenues to clarification may be given, as well as the possibility of misunderstanding and conflict, thus being broken.

The art of listening takes time, perseverance, and commendation to be able to listen to your partner profoundly. With these elements, couples will be able to change how they communicate with each other, resulting in a relationship that works based on mutual respect, understanding, and empathy. The anatomy of listening, then, is holistic and does not simply involve the ears. Still, the entire being creates a holistic experience that enhances and augments the connection between people.

PRACTICING REFLECTION AND PARAPHRASING

When it comes to couple communication, using the art of reflection and paraphrasing becomes a very effective technique that can help bring a better understanding and connection between two individuals. Such an ability demands that one should listen actively and then restate what his or her partner is saying in words, without judgment and distortion. This is not only a means to achieve clarity, but it also reduces the chances of misinterpretation, which is a problem most of the time, causing misunderstanding.

To be able to reflect and paraphrase well, couples will be advised to do exercises to acquire the skill. The next technique that is effective but simple is a summary of the story or issue of a partner. Consider an example whereby one of the partners complains that they are overworked in their house chores, and the other partner may react by saying, What I'm hearing is that you feel oppressed by the housework and you could use assistance. This brings confirmation but also provides an opportunity to open up a further conversation about the possibilities of resolutions.

It holds a high significance because it helps to develop transparency and minimizes the opportunity of the rise of a discussion. By rephrasing in your own words, a partner, the couple will be able to evade the misconceptions that might occur after not expressing his/her intentions or feelings. For example, when one of the partners declares, "I need more help around the house," it is very important to interpret this statement as a statement of need rather than a criticism of the efforts of the other partner.

Communication between people can also be improved by the inclusion of realistic suggestions in the course of the talk. A phrase such as "Let me know whether I forgot something important" or "Did I understand you correctly?" can act as a control mechanism that makes sure both sides of the relationship are familiar with each other. The given prompts facilitate communication and confirmation, which is essential in the process of keeping a healthy conversation.

One exercise that couples can practice is the so-called paraphrase swap, in which one spouse has to paraphrase a story or an issue being relayed by his or her spouse. The activity not only helps sharpen knowledge but also fosters empathy since one must be put in the place of his or her partner.

In addition, reflection and paraphrasing help to justify feelings without the need to jump into action in order to solve issues. Since it means to recognize the partner in feelings and situations and not to be ready to solve the issue, its validation habit requires acknowledgment of the emotions and experience of the partner without immediately joining the problem-solving mode. To provide an example, one can say; That must be so annoying; I see why you feel so. By speaking like that, one is affirming his/her partner and creating an encouraging environment.

Through these practices, the couples will be in a position to develop an effective and empathetic communication style. It can reveal more about emotional states and needs, and this is what will lead to a better and more complete relationship. As couples become more skilled at reflecting and paraphrasing, many couples say that as communication becomes less confrontational, it actually becomes more collaborative and ultimately healthy as the couple moves toward strengthening their bond.

VALIDATION OVER PROBLEM-SOLVING

Within the context of couple communication, one of the inherent features that would almost inevitably crop up is the fine line between validation and problem-solving. With good intentions, partners often jump into solving mode and stand up to offer solutions without first trying to know the depth of emotions of the person they are trying to help. Although such a tendency is based on caring, it might inadvertently result in a sense of being rejected or not understood.

Validation means acknowledging and affirming the feelings of your partner without immediately seeing the need to provide a solution to this situation. This strategy involves a lot of patience and the capacity to sit with unease, and gives the other person a chance to feel listened to and understood. It is not that we should agree with the point of view of our partner, but rather that we must be able to acknowledge that the feelings are meaningful and valid.

Validation may be experienced in the attitude of listening and responses that are empathetic. The best way to react when someone conveys a concern is by paraphrasing what the partner told you and getting the overall tone of what he/she feel. This could be in the form of saying, "I am told that you are struggling with the amount of work you have, and that must be difficult." These kinds of statements help express a feeling of understanding and empathy, building an environment of safe communication.

Lack of validation may, in many instances, escalate conflicts. When spouses go straight to solutions, they may appear to disregard the emotional component of the prediction. This may create a circle of communication failure: one of the partners feels he/she is not listened to, and the other is frustrated because he/she can do nothing. Couples can work on mindfulness communication techniques that are focused on validation instead of resolving a problem immediately.

A good strategy is to have a validation-only time in a conversation. During this stage, partners do not expect to provide solutions or advice, or even mention them. Unlike in the previous stages, they are meant to concentrate on listening and recognizing each other. Understandably, this practice can especially come in handy in cases concerning the negotiation of sensitive or recurrent topics where emotions may be put on the line and easy solutions may not come forth easily.

In addition to this, validation can trigger more of an emotional bond, creating stronger trust and intimacy. Validated partners will be open, share their vulnerability, and relate to each other more deeply. With time, this creates an atmosphere of trust, where each of them knows that they are safe to express themselves without any fear of disapproval or rejection.

It is also necessary to note that problem-solving cannot be excluded by validation. Instead, it preconditions more productive solutions to the problem because both partners tend to feel that they are heard and valued.

After the validation of emotions, couples are able to work together to identify solutions, and their ability to understand each other gives them an upper hand in overcoming the problems at hand.

How a person validates their relationships on a daily basis can transform the dynamic of an existing relationship. It creates a peaceful environment, understanding, and goodwill, which also forms an important part of maintaining a healthy relationship. Couples who value validation are also in a better place to cope with the intricacies of the relationship, creating an environment of support and nurturing.

Finally, validation over problem-solving is also an effective instrument when communicating with a couple. It changes the emphasis not only on merely mending cracks but on emotional attachments, that is, in the environment where both partners feel cherished and listened to. The strategy allows them to both solve conflicts more efficiently, as well as create a rich emotional fabric of the relationship that preconditions permanent growth and mutuality.

DAILY LISTENING EXERCISES

Listening is an art, and it is one of our daily practices in the world of nurturing relationships, which reminds partners of the attention and care they owe to one another. Every day is full of potentially opening up hidden opportunities, getting to know and learn from others, and creating meaningful links that previously never occurred.

Listening by definition means sinking below the level of words and taking an interest in the emotional overtones and the unsaid qualifications of speech. The step is to get the stage set--distractions are reduced to the minimum, and the environment is set favorably to open communication.

This could include identifying a peaceful space, where the noise of everyday life is non-existent, or even closing off books, computers, and televisions, so much of our time and attention have been diverted to them.

The daily exercise in listening helps the couples to establish a time on a daily basis for such practice. It is a promise to be present and interact with one another without distracting sounds from some additional activities. However, this does not have to be serious; it may as well be a few minutes while sipping morning tea or being reflective before going to bed, where both partners have the chance to talk about what went on during the day they had.

To hear is to actually listen to what one is saying. This includes maintaining eye contact, nodding, and saying things like, I see or that makes sense as a form of affirming understanding. Furthermore, it is about phrasing the questions to clarify something, rephrasing what is being said so that it is soundly understood, and showing empathy in the words and actions.

A good listening activity can be followed by repeating the instruction wording: "Tell me something which made you smile today." These types of questions not only stimulate sharing but also mindfulness on the part of the partners in appreciating the positive experiences that occurred in their relationship. In contrast to speaking about accomplishments, speaking about challenges could be done with such phrases as: What irritated you today? This allows partners to provide emotional support and understanding, which strengthens emotional connections.

These activities are not focused on problem-solving but on the creation of a free space where they can express their feelings and thoughts without fear of criticism and interruptions. It is a process of validation that is carried out daily, in which both partners feel recognized and appreciated, and their experiences and emotions are respected.

Listening exercises can be incorporated into everyday activities so as to have a gradual change in the communication pattern of a relationship. Over time, the partners may access a more powerful sense of duty in intimacy and trust, because listening can be regarded as a job, but also as a cherished thing to do. The practice teaches a partner to be attentive and reminds them that they need to rest and dedicate time to each other, which can make them relate better to one another.

Finally, the exercises can be viewed as a reminder that one is supposed to become attentive and empathetic as a habit. Their purpose is to get everyone connected, to remind each other about the love and respect that are the pillars of their alliance, and to do that every day. Listening as an everyday activity for couples can be a growth experience that leads to maintaining a thriving relationship that is also strong and capable of withstanding any challenge

CHAPTER 4

Navigating Conflict Effectively

MAPPING CONFLICT PATTERNS

It is sometimes a common situation that couples become locked in recurring cycles of conflict situations, seemingly out of thin air, but they turn out to follow a script. This knowledge of patterns is very important in turning conflict into a constructive mechanism rather than a destructive one. Noticing the distinctive cycle of arguments that every couple is going through implies exploring the relations from the inside out in the aspects that start those conflicts, promote them, and ultimately end these conflicts.

Determining the causes of the issues that trigger the disputes is one of the initial stages of mapping such patterns. It is likely to be as diverse in triggers as failed expectations, communication pitfalls, or other forms of external pressure that can supercharge any prior stresses, among others. With an obligation to keep a list of these triggers, couples are able to start noticing trends that connect their conflicts. One way to get to the practical side is to keep a conflict mapping worksheet in which you write down at least one possible argument you encounter over and over again to see where it will go in the long run.

During this exercise, couples can make notes about when the argument starts and when it escalates, as well as the effects of the argument. This systematic monitoring assists in identifying the specific times when discussions go in a terrible direction. As an example, a couple would get to know that fights often occur after dinner when not all tasks were completed, and both spouses engage in a loud voice, and the fight ends with one of them going out of the room. It is these discoveries that are important in conceptualizing the way that trivial interactions might devolve into conflicts.

Other activities which form part of the mapping process include defining the role of each partner in the conflict. This might include the understanding of whether one will chase and the other retreat, or both will escalate or nurture. These roles can be made clear by visual aids like a pursuer-distancer dynamic chart, which can prove very helpful. When couples visualize such roles, they get a picture of their role in the process of conflict and the perspective of stopping the cycle.

Comparison of these trends throughout the years not only shows all the bad loops but also gives an opportunity to reflect and develop. It prompts couples to be truthful and non-blameful after a conflict and to learn about their patterns as opposed to case-by-case events. This may include utterances in their thoughts, such as, What made us go off? or "What have we attempted to make the bridge back to connection?" These questions encourage a better appreciation of how relationship dynamics are playing out and lead to an amicable process of addressing problems.

With conflict patterns, the couples can understand how to predict conflict and avoid losing energy to fuel it. Such proactive development diverts the attention to solving conflicts towards preventing them so that couples can build a healthier dynamic of relationships. As much as we need to avoid conflict, learning and understanding these patterns is a way to use conflict as a bridge to better communication and mutual understanding.

THE 5-MINUTE PAUSE TECHNIQUE

It is easy to see how, in the context of couple communication, emotional outbursts tend to eclipse rational communication. It is perhaps important to mention that the 5-minute pause tactic could prove to be a primary tool in that turbulent water, and it is good to recognize that a brief intermission holds a lot of power. The given technique is not just about calling upon silence, but an organized method of promoting clarity and emotional control in situations of conflict.

When the human brain loses its balance because of the intense wave of emotions, it turns to its survival mode, where the intellectual part plays a passive role. This highly emotional tide is the pitfall of any intent to effect a successful communication between the partners as they begin to respond to the discussion rather than respond to it. Having a break gives both of them some distance, and it reduces the emotional charge.

The application of this technique implies that there needs to be a mutual understanding and agreement between partners. It is initiated when one of the partners is conveying a need to pause. This can be accomplished by a pre-determined utterance or a gesture, so that both individuals are aware of this as an indicator of momentary disconnection as opposed to avoidance. The silence itself is not absolute pausing but rather a short, calculated stop with a time frame of about five minutes.

The period of pause is followed by encouragement to take part in grounding activities. These could be deep breathing exercises (some may include the 4-7-8 breath technique) whereby breathing should be inhaled with a count of four, hold in seven, and then exhale after eight. Another option is a brief walk, stretching, or journaling to shift the attention and calm the mind. The trick is to use this period to think about your feelings, motives, and wider picture of the conflict in question.

The success of the pause will depend on whether it is temporary and there is a willingness to meet again. Couples are also advised to do a reading test and make sure that both people are relaxed enough to continue the process. This check-in is essential in order to re-establish the purpose of the pause- to come back to the conversation with a new clarity and with a better understanding of the other.

Once the dialogue is restarted, the environment must be less tense so that a more balanced communication might occur. Spouses should apply I statements to give each other the impression and form that they are open and understand each other. This is why the pause can be seen as a reset button that can help a couple create a shift in crossing an obstacle of reactivity towards thinking through interaction.

The technique involving 5-minute pauses in the process of communication involves patience and habitual practice. It is not a universal solution, but rather a tool that can be molded by a couple to their specific needs. In the long run, this generally becomes a good practice that would improve the emotional intelligence within the relationship through a culture of respect and people communicating mindfully.

The 5-minute pause is, on the one hand, very simple, but on the other, has a lot of depth. It gives couples the power of changing a potential conflict into an opportunity to grow and connect because it provides a well-structured means of leaving the depths of an emotional roller coaster. When applied holistically, this technique stops being an approach and turns into a kind of ritual, which forms the basis of a strong, sound-minded partnership.

DE-ESCALATION PHRASES AND SCRIPTS

During the arguing, it can become very easy to get caught in a feedback loop that makes the intensity of the argument worse. Being able to overcome this cycle is instrumental in having a healthy and productive relationship. The implementation of a set of de-escalation phrases, scripts, or, in general, a powerful toolkit can be used to help couples go through conflicts with emotions and understanding.

The so-called pause protocol is also one of the basic methods. This is a very simple yet effective solution that couples can adopt when emotions begin to run high. As an example, one of them may say, I am overwhelmed-is it possible to take a 5-minute break and resume later? This pause request is not one strategy to avoid making a decision, but a brief move back to give composure. In this break, people will have an opportunity to do some grounding exercises (including, but not limited to, deep breathing or journaling) to soothe their minds and gain a better grasp of the situation so they can resume the conversation more wisely.

After taking a break in the conversation, one should proceed with it carefully. It is important to make it clear that silence was not an instrument that could have been used to avoid the problem; rather, it allowed both partners to talk more productively. It could be as easy as checking in and then moving on: "Before we begin, we should check in--do we both feel good to go? This prepares both of you so that you have respect for each other in terms of emotional situations.

Arming couples with a series of de-escalation phrases can, in fact, change the direction of an argument and help the couple avoid a fiery argument. Such expressions as, I could see how much this means to you or "We both could use a breath before we proceed" can be used to confirm to the other person how you feel about them and to create an instance of tranquility. Misplaced humor can also be a good tension release factor. As laid-back as it may sound, the joke, as in "Alright, both of us have to behave as hangry toddlers at present," can dispel the seriousness and enable both partners to take a look at the situation with new eyes.

Nonverbal communication is also a major step in de-escalation. Even such modest indicators as a hand to be held or a smile depicting comfort may also show a wish to connect and have a common language. Establishing individualized repair attempt cues, such as a peace sign or a heart, can become a nonverbal consent in order to take a break and reconnect.

Couples are recommended to design their safe phrases or alternative words that can be used as an emergency button when there is a conflict. As an example, mentioning a word as pineapple can be a sign of mutual agreement to set the argument on hold and divert the subject of attack to the process of finding a solution. Such a habit not only individualizes the de-escalation process but also reinforces the bond in a couple.

When dealing with some of the repetitive conflicts that arise, i.e., money, in-laws, or love-making, it is important to analyze what causes these conflicts in the first place. This is because by changing the focus of the argument to the how and not the what, a couple is able to bring out even a deeper understanding of the argument. The use of curiosity-based questions such as "What does it mean to you to be financially secure?" or "How do you feel when we discuss the visits with my family?" will allow introducing the tone of fruitful communication and decreasing the chances that a conflict may emerge in the future.

The point of having these various de-escalation strategies in place is to develop an atmosphere where the partners will feel listened to and respected. Applying such tools to their communication, couples can translate the potential conflicts into development and closer contact with each other; thus, leading to more effective and less-stressed relations.

REPAIR RITUALS

It is in the complicated flows of associations and relationships where clashes are bound to occur, and how couples negotiate within troubled water is what determines how strong or weak a relationship has become. Repair rituals give a healing balm to injuries that disagreements and misunderstandings cause. Such rituals are not only about fencing-mending, but they bond a relationship that is stronger and more resilient.

Think of two people who are about to have an ostensible misunderstanding, feelings elevated, and words left unspoken or interpreted improperly. It is here that repair rituals come in, which are a systematic but non-aggressive form of reunion. They are deliberate actions aimed at the couple, a chain of steps that the couple can use to help them come back to one another. These rites are well-designed based on the dynamics involved in the relationship between two persons, so that they can be appealing to both partners.

Repair rituals wonder that there is variety and flexibility. The rituals can start from as simple as a shared glance or touch to more elaborate things like cooking a meal together to give the couple a space to express their way back to peace. It is about the performance of those moments of vulnerability and the conversion of such moments into feel-good moments. It may mean a ceremony of mutual affirmation in the darkness of the night, and to another person, it may be a playful handshake to promulgate the remaining tension.

To create such rituals, both partners have to start a discussion of what seems to be true and significant to them. It is the team effort where imagination and openness are of the essence. Couples should embrace the idea of trying to understand what behavior or actions will help them connect and feel stable. This may include brainstorming sessions where they list ideas in terms of the most joyful and peaceful activities. As time passes, they can shorten it down to a small number that shows the most potential of being useful in the successful repair.

The rituals should also change as relationships do. What was successful at the beginning of a relationship may have to be modified when the relationship becomes older and when new issues challenge it. Seasonal rituals can refresh the rituals and avoid routinization. This flexibility means that the rituals can remain functional in delivering comfort and reconnection, so that when it is needed, it will be an effective ritual.

In addition, the rituals are not only about conflict resolution but also about praising development. They help a couple remember the path that they went through as a couple and how they have grown as people and have better understood each other. Routine revisiting and reconsidering such rituals help couples celebrate their achievements and correct the necessary steps to remain tuned with a still-developing relationship.

In a nutshell, repair rituals can make an effective difference in helping couples overcome conflict and create a connection. They are a symbol of how strong and committed love is and how much people are devoted to raising a relationship. As a couple commits their time and energy to establishing and upkeeping these rituals, they will build a solid base of trust and understanding; thus, despite the most difficult weather conditions, they will be able to weather all together. Couples manage to reinforce their relationship by going through these rituals because, in the process, they are able to mend the fissure in their relationship and strengthen the bond; therefore, it becomes stronger and more lasting.

CHAPTER 5

Expressing Vulnerability Safely

UNDERSTANDING VULNERABILITY

In the context of sexual life, vulnerability is typically viewed as one of the terrifying phenomena, but it is also the factor that creates truly profound relationships. Being vulnerable means being open enough to reveal to another person the darkest corners of your mind, and the most dreadful fears and the deepest desires, and it is, in a way, a form of risk-taking, but also a key to true intimacy.

To know about being vulnerable, he or she should first realize the fears that tend to occur when opening up. People are afraid to open up about their real identity due to the fear of being rejected, judged, or misunderstood. However, being vulnerable can help the two partners to shatter the emotional boundaries in a relationship and get closer to each other to understand one another more deeply.

Becoming vulnerable consists of steps. It begins by admitting the little things, e.g., talking about mundane frustrations or pleasures. Once trust is established, it is safe to venture into deeper issues where the partners may share fears or dreams they have had. This gradual method assists in curbing the fear that the vulnerability may trigger, hence the weakness. This makes it easy to practice and gain less fear in taking such practices.

There must also be a favorable environment for vulnerability. These discussions ought to be done in an environment with no distractions and pressures, where both sides will feel relaxed and keen to engage. It is also important to have good timing; one should not hasten conversations, but they should take place when both partners are emotionally prepared and ready to put their full effort into it.

Being vulnerable involves not only people speaking- it involves listening. It is important to accept vulnerability without making judgments about it. This involves active listening and providing support and validation from the partner. Such responses reinforce trust, thus promoting continuity in openness.

In addition, vulnerability can enhance the relationship by creating resilience. By experiencing vulnerabilities in partnership, the couples share the history of having overcome challenges, which becomes a power to strengthen their union. This meeting, somewhere on the battlefield of exhaustion, may turn a possible downfall into support for the relationship.

Said another way, emotional intimacy is an avenue through vulnerability. It brings the walls of emotional barriers with it tumbling down, and builds the banners of conviction and support. When couples learn to embrace vulnerability, they create an atmosphere in the relationship where each spouse feels respected, comprehended, and cherished as the person he/she is.

CREATING SAFE MOMENTS FOR SHARING

An important point on having a prosperous relationship is creating a safe place to share. It ensures that the environment is such that the partners feel at ease and at liberty to share their inner understanding of thoughts, feelings, and experiences without any fear of backlash. This will start with an agreement on the conceptualization of what would form a safe place in the relationship and focus on emotional license, respect, and trust as the core components.

The given situation can be visualized as follows: one of the partners is confident enough to rent a childhood experience to which his/her other half will respond with a supportive attitude, instead of mockery. Such openness entails an intention to define some ground rules that impose utmost consideration of safety and comprehension. The possibility of partners deciding about safe word mechanisms or some pre-conversation ritual (when one party says they are ready to talk about something deep) should be mentioned as an example. These rituals may involve a minute of breathing together or some short and relaxing activity that puts everyone in the right atmosphere for discussion.

The setting in which these talks occur is also quite determinant. It is also recommended that a proper time and place be chosen where there are no distractions and interruptions, so that input on the quality of the communication becomes very high. This could entail making out some time of the week in order to communicate, ensuring both members are available and willing to converse, or making a no-devices area of privacy in order to do so, to eliminate any possible diversion.

Still, such things as making a safe space should not be a once-off but an ongoing practice. Frequent checks between the couples can maintain an environment like this, so-called safety check-ins that are used to reiterate the promise to communicate equally and openly. These check-ins are a chance to get rid of any problems that could have emerged and find ways so that both spouses can feel understood and listened to.

Another important aspect is the personalization of the meaning of emotional safety. Each person has his or her needs, and what feels safe to one person may not be safe to another. Prodding both partners to share their ideas about what emotional safety entails is important, as it enables the pair to construct the communication dynamics in the partnership to suit both individuals. For example, one partner may need verbal reassurance after being vulnerable, yet the other one may need time to process the information.

This sense of safety can be nurtured or unraveled through particular conduct. Maintaining eye contact and nodding (as well as an open posture) could be used to emphasize trust, with sarcasm or flippant gestures being able to destroy trust in an instant. Creating a zone in which all judgments and criticisms can be put on hold is needed, and both partners should agree to avoid defensiveness even during a challenging conversation.

This process can also be facilitated by reflection exercises, which require the couples to reminisce on what has occurred when they either felt safe or unsafe in an emotional context. Through such observations, partners are able to determine what strategies worked and what did not, meaning that they are likely to be able to interact better next time.

The aspect of inclusivity in communication is also essential, and each of the partners should have their background, identity, and experiences acknowledged and respected. The show of this respect may be made in very minor ways, such as addressing the proper pronouns or upholding cultural heritage and a belief of belonging and acceptance in the relationship.

After all, making a safe space to share is a shared responsibility and a long-term commitment. Both partners should care about preserving such an environment, as they should realize that development and bonding are a mutual process requiring constant cultivation.

SCRIPTS FOR SHARING DESIRES AND DOUBTS

With the fragile balance of relationship dynamics, the art of communication when it comes to expressing wants and doubts can be quite delicate. Relationships are nearly always struggling with delicacy and discernment of how to communicate their deepest feelings, to strike that balance between fragility and self-defense. This chapter explores the dynamics of both sharing wants and worries and provides a map that couples should use when they communicate what they want and desire more clearly and compassionately.

The core of successful communication is the possibility to state desires without feeling guilty or blaming. Most people have past experiences, and as a result, it becomes a burden that makes people express their needs in certain ways. Due to cultures, upbringing, and past relationships, it just might be a silent script that determines the way the requests happen. To deal with this, couples will be advised to use the linguistic device otherwise known as I statements, which focuses on the experience rather than on allegation. As an example, we could say something like the following: I get overwhelmed when

I have to do all the chores. Is it possible to talk about a more equal division of them?" Spreads out blame and blaming, and moves to work together.

In addition, guilt-free communication is also supported by guidance through scripts that marvel at what the other person says without excuse. It is easy to say something like, I would like to go out on a date night this week. Were you willing to plan one there and then? Or "Would you tell me when you were going to be late home? It makes me feel loose." These are the aspects that support the right to be understood and to be straightforward, that take the burden of apologizing or condemning the discourse.

Expressions of desires rely heavily on self-compassion. Couples are also taken through exercises and mantras that ensure that they get rid of the shame connected to asking what they want. The mere statement of words such as I have needs, and my needs are legit. It is alright to get asked, and this will give people the strength to speak up whatever they want, and they are not afraid to get judged.

Limits are also an essential element of good communication. Traditional boundaries and flexible boundaries are the ways to distinguish the differences that are hard by definition (like using no phones at dinner) and flexible by nature (let us get into finances after our kids go to bed). Boundary setting and revisiting scripts provide phrases and conversation starters that are assertive and friendly, and recognize limits.

Another pillar of sharing desires and doubts is Vulnerability. Expressing a fear or a dream would lead to increased intimacy, but there would be the chance of rejection as well. The chapter offers prompts and scripts on how the couples can be led in such vulnerable discussions. The importance of time and place is underlined; the time and place have to be well selected because then the process and the outcome of such discussions could be greatly influenced.

It is also vital that vulnerability be received in an empathetic way as opposed to defensively. Couples learn to become aware and eliminate the common defensive behaviors, including those where people cut an interception or evasion. They are rather advised to resort to the so-called pause and breathe response, which leaves room for empathetic and understanding responses. The queries, such as "Could you tell me more about how that feels to you?" may be used. Encourage more openness and show sincere interest.

The conclusion of the chapter points out that the purpose of the chapter is to offer the tool that couples can use to exchange desires and doubts with grace and understanding. With a created environment whereby both partners are free to express their needs, a relationship becomes fruitful and is established on the grounds of mutual respect and openness.

RESPONDING WITH EMPATHY

Empathy is a communication medium through which hearts get closer to each other and are able to achieve understanding and compassion with their communication partner. It is critical to answer empathetically instead of defensively when one of the partners exposes his/ her vulnerability. This understanding reaction creates a secure environment in which the two people feel listened to and appreciated, helping to prepare the couple for closer intimacy and togetherness.

The initial step is to be aware of the defensive responses that tend to occur. Such responses as being talkative, interrupting, minimizing, or diving into problem-solving mode have a tendency to close communication instead of opening it (becoming the barrier instead of a bridge). By appreciating the fact that these defensive measures are just normal responses to perceived threats, the couples can enter the conversations more thoughtfully.

One of the most effective gadgets in changing these dialogues is the pause and breathe method. This is cogitating for a short time about a response, through breathing and gathering of one's thoughts. It is not only a technique to relax the mind, but it also helps to open the heart and to listen and feel the partner. In this way, they can give answers based on an empathetic and supportive nature instead of criticism and not believing.

It is essential to model empathetic responses in the process. A phrase such as, thank you so much for telling me that, or, I think it was so brave of you to tell me that, can show the partner a great deal of respect and appreciation for the way they feel. Such reactions indicate that the feelings expressed by the partner are also acceptable and deserve consideration, thus making further disclosure and confidence even more appealing.

Follow-up questions are essential in order to elaborate on the understanding. An open question, such as "Can you give me more information about how that feels to you?" asks the partner to discuss the feelings, and a deeper communication rather than shallow exchanges will emerge. Such an exercise not only contributes to better knowledge but also serves to show interest in the subjective world of the partner.

Presence, in addition to words, is also a sign of empathy in communication. Communication with a partner is supported by non-verbal signals that he is interested and responsive, such as eye contact, nodding, and a relaxed attitude. These hints can say a lot and can tell more than words themselves may convey in expressing empathy and understanding.

In addition to this, practicing and being mindful of developing the habit of replying to someone in an empathetic manner is necessary. The exercises to make couples more empathetic can include role-playing games in which a couple listens and responds without giving any advice or solutions. It can be used to build the muscle of empathy, so it is natural to communicate using it.

When one of the partners believes that he/she should tell about some fears or insecurity, support with empathy can be made to change the character of the relationship in moments of weakness. It changes the emphasis in problem-solving to connecting, fixing, and comprehending. Such an empathetic approach not only helps to reinforce the connection between the partners but also creates a context in which both feel safe to communicate freely and be their genuine selves.

After all, the ability to be empathetic is all about being more emotionally focused than having to be concerned with what is being said. It is more concerned with just being there through an open-hearted listening and a non-hurried affirmation of the partner without immediately offering solutions. This compassionate attitude leads to a more flexible, stronger bond that can sustain the pressures that are experienced in living together.

CHAPTER 6

Building Rituals for Connection

DAILY CONNECTION RITUALS

A little effort and regular attention can be made to weave a durable tapestry of bonds in the dance of relationships. Though these rituals might appear trivial to a great extent, they are the strings that connect couples and build a feeling of companionship and of knowing one another. What daily connection rituals are all about is the fact that these rituals turn banal situations into chances of emotional connection and development.

Just think of how you can wake up every day and practice gratitude. The partners do not forget to say something positive and recognize something done by the other partner, like making coffee or speaking a few comforting words the previous day. Although this is not a long ritual, it fosters a good mood as it creates a positive note of gratitude and mutual respect that can reverberate throughout the rest of the day. With the help of gratitude, couples develop both a feeling of resilience and emotional closeness that have been shown scientifically to improve relationships based on satisfaction.

At night, a few minutes of checking in before going to bed can act as a tender way to close a day. This is a way in which the couple gets to spend time together and share a special event of their day, a worry, or a mere emotion they are feeling. These check-ins will not solve any problems but provide a secure environment to share and listen, and that will strengthen the notion that each partner feels valued and comprehended. These micro-moments of connection help cut off everything that could build up sentiments of grievance and misunderstandings, making way for emotional connections on an additional level.

Digital communication is a curse and a blessing to couples who have to struggle against contemporary life. A digital detox can help them improve the quality of their interactions when they add it to their routine. Putting aside particular hours when the screen is off, such as lunch, dinner, or bedtime, promotes in-person contact, minimizes distractions, and lets partners be there in the sense of giving full attention to each other with no distractions.

Another way connection can be achieved is through the use of play and humor in daily rituals. Mutual joking and humor can defuse any tension between both of you and keep you close to each other, both in spirit and physically, as both of you enjoy being together and having fun. Spontaneous dance party in the kitchen or fun two-step over the best pancake maker, these sorts of levity moments are like a reset button, breaking the repetitiveness and stress of day-to-day life.

Besides, the bond could be strengthened by forming individualized rituals that show the dynamics of the relationship. Spouses may come up with their specific farewell in the morning, or can establish a weekly meal by preparing a different dish together. Such rituals not only deepen bonding but also provide a feeling of security and permanence that ties the relationship to events and experiences that make up collective memories.

In the end, the main strength of rituals of daily connection is their ease and regularity. They do not need big things or a lot of time spent; they have an intention of making a connection in the midst of the busy life of daily living. Integrating these practices through experiencing them in everyday life, the couples will be able to build their healthy, happy, and strong relationship where both of them feel important, listened to, and valued. These are the day-to-day gestures of connection that constitute the silent yet powerful bond that creates the basis of relationship development.

WEEKLY CHECK-IN PRACTICES

When considering the sphere of cultivating intimate relationships, the habit of checking up on each other on a regular basis becomes a rather powerful means of building a bond and improving the knowledge of one another. It is a scenario when one takes a break from the routine and mutually explores feelings, intentions, and reflections. This religious time, although it may appear a simple thing, is aimed at avoiding the unnoticed accumulation of resentment and at achieving a higher emotional responsiveness between a man and a woman.

Think of a Sunday night, when the week provides a natural break. Couples are seated, probably with a hot beverage in their hands, and they are involved in what one might call a state-of-the-union talk. This is not a meeting but an arena where the partners recollect the past week and stipulate desires about the following days. The strength of these rather well-organized, yet loose interactions can be explained by their periodicity and constructive atmosphere that they provide to speak freely. These times are not concerned with performance reviews but are concerned with true connection, and to do that, one has to ask the question, How are we truly doing? Became a regular question.

In order to start and regularly maintain such check-ins, couples can start by using some easy prompts. What is one good thing that happened to us this week? Or "Is there anything you wish it had been done differently?" functions as a mild opening to further discussion. Such basic questions are on the surface, but they lead to a healthy conversation, and both sides of the relationship are able to know that they are understood and respected.

Such check-ins require a safe environment to flourish. Think of turning the lamps down, lighting a candle, or preparing a beloved morsel as instances of ritual that serve to mark the start of this lustful engagement. These rituals allow for the creation of an atmosphere of peace and concentration and tell that this is something out of the ordinary, that this is a special moment that cannot be mixed with other things happening in the real world. Ground rules such as switching off phones and sitting to face each other create the sense of having a good listening so that both partners can give all of themselves.

These routines are easy to work on and encourage any couple to bring more creative concern to the personalization of these rituals and make check-ins something special to both parents. Others may appreciate a walk-and-talk check-in, where walking together will help loosen up a conversation that flows naturally and comfortably. On some level, an outdoor emoji check-in text could provide a fun but practical aspect of sharing emotions on a busy day with others.

Introducing the element of gratitude to these times can add to the relationship even more. Simple ways to express what each partner likes about the other partner, whether in words or small ways, help to fortify the positive feelings and build the relational bonds. The act of appreciation could be as easy as a text in the morning or an appreciation at night, but what is important is ensuring that the emphasis remains on the qualities and behaviors that make the relationship better.

Finally, it is always about the spirit of weekly check-ins to develop a beat of introspection and intimacy. This is used to remind people that relationships need to be attended to and nurtured constantly, similar to a garden. These endeavors actually mean that in doing them, the couples are not simply sustaining their relationship, but are actually cultivating it effectively, making sure that it continues to be rich in life and healthy and able to resist the vicissitudes of life.

CELEBRATING MILESTONES

In this dynamic process of relationships, the light and enthusiasm can be commemorating milestones and being happy with them. By sharing and celebrating accomplishments, large or small, couples strengthen the ties that bind them. This recognition not only drives motivation but also roots the relationship and can provide a history of successes that need to be revisited in the bad moments.

Just think of how wonderful it is to arrive at a breakthrough in the communication process after months of trying. It could be the very first time either partners negotiate a hard discussion without reverting to the old habit of blame or defense. These are the moments that are worth celebrating, not just because they are a peaceful time, but also because they indicate growth.

Recording such milestones, couples appreciate the path they have been moving together and how far they have come.

The parties do not need to be big. It is not the process of getting festive but the process of being festive that makes one joyful and strengthens the positive change. It can be as simple as a high-five after a good check-in or having a special meal to celebrate how one managed to work out a difficult conversation. Such minor signs of celebration form positive feedback, which increases growth and develops the relationship between partners.

Couples are also advised to keep a record of their victories, which can be done by maintaining a journal of relationship victories or by updating a close friend or therapist. Voice memos to yourself on what you are proud of and/or writing about the small things that have gone right this week can be a very effective way to remember how far you have progressed already. The practice helps not only to build the relationship but also to have physical evidence of the progress that can be revisited in case of any doubts or challenges.

Another important feature of the celebration of milestones is reflection. Couples are expected to make it a habit to stop and evaluate what has been going well in the relationship. Incorporating questions such as, What is one thing we did better this month, and What is a new micro-habit we would like to start this coming month? It can aid in pinpointing trends and establishing intentions to be achieved. The contemplative exercise will create an atmosphere of constant improvement and will make sure that the relationship changes and evolves.

In addition, milestones are not limited to positive accomplishments. Fighting with struggles, despite crises, or just struggling together to survive through the tough times is equally something to celebrate. Such times of survival represent how solid and rich a relationship is; thus, the day when a couple proves their dedication and persistence.

As it is, commemorating milestones in a relationship is not so much about the milestone event. It is a habit that instills a sense of appreciation, enforces and embraces positive behavior, and, in addition, builds the emotional bond between the partners. It also recognizes the hard work, endurance, and commitment that both individuals engage in so that the partnership can work. As entities of important celebrations incorporated into the fabric of everyday life, couples are producing a tapestry of experiences that sustain the relationships and provide a source of constant growth.

GRATITUDE SHARING

Gratitude sharing has become one of the key rituals in the area of building and maintaining a healthy relationship. It is something very small and at the same time deep that can change the interaction between the partners. A daily gratitude practice aids in generating a feeling of gratitude, increasing emotional strength, and relationship satisfaction overall. It is a scientifically mixed practice that urges couples to identify and tells them to say positive things about their partner and the relationship, hence developing a positive emotional atmosphere.

The practice requires committing to spending a little, daily, consistent time by way of thanking an individual partner. This could go as far as a single step that says something you liked about your partner during the day. It might be something considerate, something encouraging, or just the mere fact that you acknowledge that they are there and exist in your life. It can be implemented and practiced in a face-to-face format or digitally, in the form of a text message, which will provide the necessary flexibility and adaptability of the practice to the lifestyle of the couples.

To go through with this daily process of gratefulness, couples may be advised to find a time that best suits both of them, as long as they always have the time, be it during dinner, right before bed, or even first thing in the morning. It is possible to create a routine to make this practice become a regular way of interacting between the couple. The trick is to keep these expressions largely honest and, in particular, to be more than generic appreciation, to point out exactly what behavior or character is valued. For example, "I thought it was great how you spent time listening to me regarding my concerns today," or "Thanks very much, as you made my favorite dinner tonight, it felt good that I am special." These exact graces not only show appreciation but also strengthen desirable behavior and help create a supportive relationship climate.

Couples will also want to add the element of surprise by using gratitude weeks or sometimes a gratitude surprise. This can be something like leaving gratitude notes around the most unexpected spots, coming up with a common gratitude jar to check before a difficult day, or something like coming up with a theme, such as gratitude towards acts of service or gratitude towards emotional support, as an example, which can be used for a week. Such differences assist in maintaining the originality of the ritual and its interests.

Further, gratitude sharing must be discussed as a two-way bonanza in which both partners would take turns in sharing it with equal participation. One needs to feel that both individuals are equally met and appreciated, and this gives a sense of balance and respect. When both partners practice it, the bond is not only strengthened, but there is a source of good feelings that could be tapped into in other harsher moments.

Essentially, gratitude sharing is not just a practice to be followed every day, but rather a daily practice to be given to another. It is all about creating an appreciation-based framework that can be used to develop and maintain the relationship throughout the highs and lows. Couples who continuously practice gratitude on purpose and make it a frequent, ongoing practice will foster closer bonding between each other and a stronger relationship. It is a small but effective exercise that reminds us of the goodness in others and reminds them why they fell in love and committed to one another in the first place.

CHAPTER 7

Adapting Communication Across Stages

EARLY RELATIONSHIP COMMUNICATION

At the initial stages of a relationship, things usually go well concerning communication, powered by the hype of knowing a stranger. The first stage can be described as an exuberance to share, to hear, and to know the other person, the stories, the dreams, the freakish bindings. Communicating partners tend to have long and significant discussions due to the fact that they share their history, interests, and ambitions. Thus, this builds a basis of mutual curiosity and interest.

However, in reality, there are some obstacles to this natural flow of communication as it is encountered with the growth of any relationship beyond the honeymoon. The exuberance of early times may even lead to complacency, and what was once a flowing exchange of ideas may have to be given some deliberate attention. Initial communication issues in relationships are, therefore, a crucial stage of setting up patterns that will tend to shape the long-term functioning of the couple.

One of the initial things that a couple has to struggle through is the issue of striking a balance between remaining an individual and fostering togetherness. The two partners come into the relationship with experiences and cultural backgrounds that lead to differing views, likes, dislikes, and communication styles. Early recognition and admiration of these differences can prevent incidents of failure to understand one another and even foster a stronger bond. The stage allows the couples to express their values freely, including what they would like to be communicated and what is not communicated in an open manner, which establishes the tone further down the road.

In addition, the beginning is a great period for developing good communication habits. Setting up routines like trusty check-ins would ensure there are no closed borders, as minimal problems do not transform into raging conflicts. Such check-ins do not have to be official, and they might go as basic as spending a couple of minutes daily to discuss what the other has done or heard something new. Such practice will not only support the habit of open communication but also enable the spouses to become sensitive to the emotional needs of their partner.

Conflict is a part of any relationship, and how one communicates at the initial stages of the relationship might help it or make it stronger. Couples who get to grasp positive ways of approaching conflicts early on tend to be better prepared to cope with the challenges they will face ahead. This entails being an active listener, and each partner will consciously make an effort to listen and actually hear and understand the other partner without automatically reacting to solutions and defense. It also involves training on how to communicate using words and body language to express feelings. It needs to be done in a non-accusing and respectful way, as well as in bringing about solutions as opposed to winning an argument.

The modern era of digital life introduces a next level of communication at an early stage of relations since texting and social media communication are the links added to the means of couples' communication. It is imperative to talk about digital boundaries and expectations, e.g., how often should we text, share on social media, or have digital privacy? Such dialogues can avoid any confusion and establish trust so that both partners feel happy and safe in their online interactions.

After all, effective communication in early relationships is about the establishment of a firm basis that would enable future growth and strength. Since every relationship is subject to its ups and downs, couples can be supportive, loving, caring, and understanding of each other much more when they create a climate of openness, understanding, and appreciation. The creation of such habits and frameworks at the beginning of the relationship is not only the process of addressing current communication problems, but also creating the environment of a long-term, fulfilling relationship.

SUSTAINING LONG-TERM PARTNERSHIPS

In stable relationships, communication would likely be a problem over time due to the natural tendency to drift. Couples often get on autopilot as they find themselves focused on careers, children, aging parents, and assume they know what their spouse is thinking or feeling. Such an assumption may foster emotional distancing, where the partners will cease questioning/interacting with each other.

The only thing that can be done about this drift is to nurture curiosity and emotional intimacy. It is also good that they provide rituals and questions that would allow a couple to get to know one another again. An example of this could be taking part in activities such as playing the game of 20 Questions with long-term couples, as it brings in a new spark of discovery. This is a setup that makes the partners learn something new about each other, even after years of interacting with each other.

Also, progressive reconstruction and restoration activities are driven by exercising a healthy relationship. These include the resurrection of past injuries and the renegotiating of long-lasting contracts. The relationship audit can be a worksheet that can be of value in this process, and this helps couples to systematically look at what works and what should be changed. The regular meeting (monthly) is called a state-of-the-union, where the health of the relationship is discussed, given, and taken as reflected in successes and challenges as well.

Another thing that helps maintain long-term relationships is celebrations, such as celebrating milestones and growth. It takes a special effort to remind the couples to celebrate their anniversaries, the challenges conquered, and new ambitions should be made together. As a couple, one could create an "accomplishments timeline," which will be visual evidence of the triumphs as a duo and the path that has been traveled jointly. Relationship birthdays can also be ritualized to give a humorous means of celebrating how the partnership has changed over the years.

Communication can go awry, especially when there is distance or crisis. It can be caused by physical distance, emotional turmoil, sickness, or betrayal, but these are times that have to be navigated. Some common responses, like mistrust or withdrawal, can cause unwillingness to reconnect. Commodified re-institution of the feeling of trust and emotional safety must be systematized. Physical and emotional distance caused by separation may be partially overcome through special activities such as the so-called "Daily two-minute eye contact" activity or exchanging the so-called "what I missed about you" lists.

Responding to pain, regrets, or ambiguities calls for the use of language that does not ignore the problem, but gives hope instead. Magic lines such as the one that goes, I understand that things have taken a different direction, but I would like to give it a second chance with you, which can be the start of healing talks. The rebuilding of intimacy should be a gradual process, and the small milestones that we can celebrate on the way to reconnecting (lighting a candle every night to symbolize the recommitment or going through the effort of a new shared playlist that will signify this new journey) are key to success.

Finally, long-term partnerships are all about long-term development and change. It also means knowing when communications have dried up to a point and doing something about it to give them a new life. Incorporating the specific behaviors and activities that support curiosity, celebration, and renewal, a couple can stay openly and powerfully in touch with each other and avoid fading over time.

RECONNECTING AFTER DISTANCE

Sometimes, life develops a divide between a couple, and in such a scenario, relationships are said to have a landscape. Separation can be occasioned by the physical distance, emotional distance, or post-disaster effects, and they may put to the test the stability of the relationship. Couples can be in a position to go through a post-deployed military, or they can endure the distance of their commitments with each other, or they might even be recovering from intense issues like betrayal. The situations are unique in that they keep testing the strength and depth of a relationship between two people.

The initial work goes into accepting the breach and its effect. Suspicion, reticence, and the overwhelming nature of attempting to revive the communication channels are some of the challenges. Under such circumstances, couples can feel as if they are strangers, and communication between them is stilted and cautious. It is important to recognize these barriers as the next step forward. It is not a matter of going back, but it is like raising something from the remains, out of the pieces which are left.

In order to make this fragile process a little easier, guided routines can prove to be very useful. Simple actions such as making consistent two-minute eye contact may be used to restore the trust. This discipline also welcomes couples to find a reconnection so they can see one another again and recapture the familiarity and intimacy that may have faded away. Furthermore, building communal lists of what I missed about you is a positive reinforcement, and building on positive is a way of letting partners concentrate on what was strong and positive and drew him or her to his or her partner in the first place.

To overcome pain or regret or even confusion, something beyond words is needed. Scripts can assist these challenging discussions. As an example, the desire to give it another go could be presented as the following: I know I changed, but I want to give it another go with you. This provides an avenue of communication, which opens up the road to honesty and vulnerability constructively and securely. Moreover, it would be revolutionary to know the actions that every partner can take to feel safe. Such questions as, What do you need to feel safe with me now? Assist in customizing behavior in regard to the emotional needs of one another.

The process of reconnection takes time. It has something to do with living small wins, which are important in the reconstruction of intimacy and collective meaning. Simple rituals that can make a difference and help to see progress and intent can be as simple as burning a candle each night as a recommitment or creating a new shared playlist. The acts are reminders of the synergizing trip and the new story being inscribed.

After all, reconnecting over distance is all about establishing new neural pathways of comprehension and adoration. It is truly a reflection of the pure strength of two people and their desire to work on their relationship despite the odds. It is not a linear process but one in which steps are taken towards the eventual renewal of the partnership. Couples should press on with tolerance, sympathy, and readiness to adopt a new change to turn distance into an experience of growth and strengthen their bonds.

BLENDED FAMILY DYNAMICS

Within the complex net of relationships that characterize blended families, a vital component in this web is communication, as an element towards achieving a state of harmony, as well as an understandable relationship. Such families tend to face certain special issues, as various parenting styles, the history of families, and different desires meet and form quite an original environment that needs to be negotiated properly.

The core of a blended family situation is the necessity of open, comprehensive dialogue. This includes taking into consideration the various backgrounds and experiences that all the different individuals in the family possess. Blending families is not a physical act of cohabitation but involves the incorporation, or rather the syncing of various values, cultures, and expectations. Every member, be it parent, stepparent, or child, has his/her point of view which should be respected and understood.

Loyalty binds are one of the main problems of blended families. Children, in particular, can be placed in a very conflicting situation between birth parents and stepparents, causing conflicts and misperception. Parents must share such feelings in an open, unfinalized manner that should encourage children to express freely in a place where they neither face judgment. This may be supported by regular family meeting time, which should not only allow the parents to share their minds but also allow all members to open up with their concerns. These meetings may contribute to the development of the feeling of unification and common purpose, which is necessary to ensure that a blended family is going to work adequately.

Besides loyalty ties, different parenting preferences are also a challenge experienced by blended families. It is not rare when the biological parents and stepparents disagree in discipline, education, or responsibilities at home. The best way out of these differences is to approach them in terms of respectful and constructive dialogue that seeks a common ground. Creating definitive family rules and agreements may assist in uniting parenting styles and maintaining a similar tone in the way things are handled so as to be equal, and this is imperative in providing a stable environment for kids.

The next area of serious concern in the context of blended families is the ex-partner relationship. Having a friendly and co-operative actual acquaintance with a former mate can go a long way towards influencing the emotional well-being of the children. Parents should also demonstrate respectful ways of communication and not criticize the ex-partner in front of the children. This goes a long way towards mitigating conflict as well as ensuring the children have an added feeling of security and stability.

The rituals and traditions also matter in having a sense of belonging to blended families. One way is to build a common family culture by creating new family traditions that make use of some aspects of the background of each family member. Be it a weekly game night, a special holiday event, or just a family dinner, these rituals have the potential to make a lasting imprint and bind them together.

Communication in a blended family stands on the edge of the success or failure of this family. One must show a lot of patience, understanding, and accept the change. With the focus on open communication and respect towards one another, blended families can find their way through the intricacies of their relationships and convert their possible problems into prospects for improvement. With the help of conscious work and dedication, such families will be able to establish a nurturing atmosphere where all the members will feel cherished and appreciated.

CHAPTER 8

Cultural and Personality Differences

RECOGNIZING COMMUNICATION STYLES

When communicating as a couple, it is crucial to understand that there is a lot of variety in how the partners converse. Both partners have a different combination of history, personality, and behavior that they have learned and apply to the association of the relationship, and hence, how they communicate. The knowledge and recognition of such styles of communication can also add a lot to the quality of a relationship, leading to understanding another person, avoiding misunderstandings, and establishing better contact.

Among the key points about the understanding of communication styles, it is possible to distinguish the idea that not all people can process and communicate their thoughts and emotions in the same way. Others are more communicative and expressive; they are called verbal processors. Such people are more bookish and they like talking out of their heads to sort out their ideas and emotions. The flow of words is the typical feature of their communication style because ideas are shared openly and enthusiastically. They tend to speak highly of dynamic and interactive dialogue, where they are able to feel most close to it when engaged in stimulating conversation.

Conversely, other people can be more introspective and like to think and deal with what is in their mind before they say something to the rest of the world. These people may be more introverted as they think more, ponder over what they think, and add to it. They tend to communicate more judiciously and carefully, and are not very interested in the amount. They can also be more comfortable with alone time to collect their thoughts prior to discussing them with another person, as it brings them peace of mind and clarity.

Moreover, some individuals tend to prefer non-verbal communication, as body language, facial expressions, and gestures are an important part of it. This type of presentation can communicate emotions and intentions through smooth non-verbal signs, without using words, and can be very effective. A reassuring pat on his arm, a comforting smile, and reassuring eye contact can mean so much to these people and sometimes say more than words could express.

An awareness of these diverse styles entails taking care to oversee and comprehend the intricacies in each other's communication. It is the ability to listen not merely to what is spoken but also in the manner in which it is spoken. This will involve paying attention to tone, tempo, and body language that follows the verbal message. It is through listening to such cues that spouses and couples get to know more about what each of them prefers and needs in order to create a more comfortable connection.

In addition, it is vital to know the communication style that he or she uses and its interaction with that of the partner. Self-awareness permits people to justify their strengths and weaknesses and be more understanding and patient during the process of communication. It promotes the spouses to become flexible and change their ways of communication to be more compatible with one another and to become more inclusive and helpful.

Lastly, the point in identifying communication styles is not to label or to stereotype the partners into pre-determined categories. Rather, it is on embracing the differences in the ways they express themselves, and it is on seeing these differences as an opportunity to grow, connect, and appreciate what is held in variance with others. By establishing a culture in which every communicative style can flourish and be appreciated, married couples can establish a more durable, robust, and stronger connection that takes into consideration the peculiarities of the inputs of the partners in a communication process. This awareness opens up the path to more fulfilling interactions, as both partners are being heard, understood, and appreciated.

BRIDGING CULTURAL GAPS

Communication is the foundation of any relationship, and when there are cultural differences involved, this becomes an even more delicate issue to navigate, with great sense and awareness. Cultural differences may present themselves in unnoticeable but quite effective ways when it comes to couple communication by affecting the ways in which they may express their feelings, solve their conflicts, and even see the surrounding world. These diversities are usually based on various cultural backgrounds, and a deliberate commitment is needed to connect so that the partnership is harmonized and enriched.

Among the key elements of managing cultural gaps in relationships, there is the need to understand that cultural differences may significantly influence the ways of communication between various cultures. An example is when certain cultures believe in direct communication and expressive verbal encounter, a culture may profess indirect communication but rely heavily on non-verbal communication and the situation. Learning about these variances is crucial so that couples do not ruin themselves in times of misunderstanding, which may result in a conflict or aloof feelings.

Partners should thus have frank discussions and explore their cultural frameworks as well as the communication parameters that they have always been familiar with, so as to fill such lapses. This is done not only by exchange of personal expectations and experiences but also by listening to whatever the other person says without approaching them with a judging attitude. These discussions will bring to the fore possible points of difference and may present an avenue through which the differences could be handled wisely.

In addition, couples are able to join in the development of the common language that takes into consideration both cultures. This does not imply coming up with a completely different language, but rather that there should be a common ground upon which both partners feel listened to and understood. This would include coming to an understanding of some words or non-verbal cues which would indicate certain feelings or intentions, and therefore cut down misunderstanding.

Cultivating curiosity and respect for one another's cultures and traditions is another important strategy that should be put in place. Sharing our cultural heritage will allow us to turn the possible barriers into a source of growth and even closer bonding. This may include engaging in some cultural practices jointly, educating one another about the kind of culture they practice, or even observing cultural holidays as two individuals. These common experiences not only enhance that relationship but also establish a more unified partnership.

We also have to mention the role of family and community expectations that may frequently impact the way cultural differences are perceived and handled in a relationship. Couples can be in a situation where they face threats or demands from family members with conservative attitudes. In such cases, couples are expected to support each other by putting boundaries and making those known to their respective families, ensuring the relationship is prioritized.

Moreover, one should understand that cultural stereotypes are likely to interfere with the communication between couples. These stereotypes may induce biases and prejudices that come in the way of veritable comprehension and empathy. Couples can also get to know each other better by keeping an open mind and being willing to receive and challenge each other's set beliefs about each other.

In the end, cultural differences in relationships have to be handled by means of tolerating, paying attention to the needs of others and their lifestyles, and engaging in ongoing learning and adaptation. As the partners make their way through these complexities, they not only develop better skills in their communication process, but they also make their relationship rich in the various possibilities and extensive enrichment each culture can include. By relating to each other and respecting one another, couples will be able to turn the cultural disparities into stepping stones to a more gratifying and successful relationship.

NEURODIVERSITY IN RELATIONSHIPS

The neurodiversity is another added reflection in the relationship dance with unique challenges and rewarding growth opportunities. Frequently, couples find themselves in a situation where they have to manage the regulation of diverse neurotypes, and it might be ADHD or autism that has a profound effect on communication style, emotional needs, and relationship comprehension. Becoming conscious of these differences is more important not as a challenge to be dealt with but rather as different capabilities that can further enrich connections among people.

Different partners in neurodiversity relationships often have to face differences in communication and speed. To make sense of an example, one of the partners may be verbal and fast at processing the information. In contrast, another partner may take some time and may prefer written communication because he or she can better understand it. By learning about these differences, we can avoid much misunderstanding and become patient and understanding. It is advised that couples work towards ensuring such an environment is created so that both partners can be at ease discussing their needs without the fear of being judged and/or being brisk.

Flexibility and creativity could play a great role in improving the communication between them. Longer processing time when conversations take place or when using written notes can assist in ensuring that the exchange is clear, so that misunderstandings are avoided. Such modifications also prove to be adaptations to neurotypes. Still, they also pay strong attention to the individual mode of one partner experiencing the world, which is also respected in such a way.

Another crucial ingredient of the neurodiverse relationship success is celebrating the strengths of each partner that we can bring to the table. The partners are also urged to understand and value one another, using different listening styles and ways of solving problems. It is an acknowledgment which can be life-affirming and life-enhancing, and where similarities as perceived become the basis of bridging and increasing. A couple of exercises may be used to help couples look back in history to when their differing styles meshed together perfectly, resulting in a positive communication interaction or problem-solving.

The other level of neurodiverse relationships is dealing with sensory sensitivities or triggering things. Partners need to speak freely about these triggers and come up with a good way to deal with them. This can include establishing sensory-friendly areas at home or establishing some signals to use in situations of overwhelmingness. This kind of practice not only remains comforting but also establishes a foundation of safety and trust.

Furthermore, the concept of having a neurodiverse relationship implies that it requires a lifetime of learning and adjustments. By finding resources and support networks that provide information on how to handle neurodiverse dynamics, couples will have an opportunity to change their patterns and come up with a better alternative. The involvement in communities or support groups around neurodiversity can be helpful in gathering understanding, having a sense of belonging, and gaining knowledge.

After all, the ability to maintain a neurodiverse relationship does not depend on it; being eager to see the difference as a virtue is the only difference. With the help of a culture of patience, understanding, and free communication, partners can turn the conflicts that arise into valuable experiences, strengthening their union. This walk not only helps couples to evolve as individuals but also helps them to connect even more to each other, building a strong and enjoyable partnership that rejoices in the beauty of diversity.

CELEBRATING DIFFERENCES

In the sphere of relation, the beauty of individuality frequently turns into a ground of development and a closer bond. Having an understanding of the individual qualities and outlooks of both partners can completely change the nature of how husbands and wives communicate into something that can be turned into a source of vitality and knowledge rather than a source of pointless misunderstanding. This process of recognition starts with one of the most fundamental, complicated phenomena of recognizing the other, in their whole fulness, not only in what they share and deem to be important to themselves, but also in what they represent to each other: differences.

Partners enhance intimacy by shifting their attitude towards differences when they take time to find out about their differences without judgment. It includes enquiry and discussion of questions that may not otherwise be the discourse of the day. It is a matter of inquiry into what customs are significant, what values were defined by the experiences of the past, and how the past experiences are implicated in current decisions. These conversations have the power to open up new dimensions of a partner that one did not understand or ever give care or attention to, and this creates a feeling of intimacy and understanding as well as camaraderie.

In order to be successful in celebrating differences, it is important that couples can create such an atmosphere in which they can feel free and express their ideas and emotions without being afraid of rejection or mockery. Validation and active listening help in creating this holding environment. As one of the partners is sharing a thought or a feeling, the other partner can paraphrase what was said/heard, which enables the partner to be sure that he (or she) has received and appreciated the message shared. Such a practice not only avoids miscommunication but also gives respect to the views of each of the partners.

When it comes to life, in the real sense of the word, celebrating differences can be incorporated into everyday life by having common rituals and routines that gaze at the unique nature of each partner. This can involve preparing foods of the other culture, participating in the other culture's interests, or even making some time to get to know more about the other culture. These activities are to remind people that though partners may pursue different paths, they always do it together and make their journeys richer, with new experiences and knowledge.

Further, celebrating differences is not only accepting what makes each one of us something special, but also what the differences bring in terms of development. The difference in the view of each partner can encourage the other person to think outside of the box, to reevaluate assumptions, and to broaden his or her horizons. Such challenges can lead to the growth of personal and more robust partnerships when approached with a free, open mind and treated with respect.

The essence of commemoration of differences is the steadfastness to continuous conversation and respect towards one another. With the complexities of their relationship, navigating through the complexities of the relationship will require constant conversation that deals with what arises out of their differences, both in terms of what propels them and what challenges them when it comes to their relationship with others. In such a way, they not only get to know one another better but also strengthen the connection, as a result of which they end up having a dynamic as well as a longstanding relationship.

After all, the fact that we celebrate differences in a relationship is a statement on how love can drive us beyond the shallowness and the banal. It is a quest towards a deeper intimacy, and the partners do not just accept but celebrate these special gifts each brings to the relationship and form a sumptuous tapestry of a mutual life and love.

CHAPTER 9

Digital Communication Strategies

SETTING DIGITAL BOUNDARIES

The ability to read the fine print of creating boundaries in the online context is imperative to couples who want to remain in balance and togetherness in our day and age, when close examination of faces through the digital lens feels as natural as being in one another's eyesight used to be. The omnipresence of smartphones, social media, and messaging programs, on the one hand, provides unlimited possibilities in communication, but on the other hand, creates certain specific problems that can break the dynamics of relationships if they are not addressed thoroughly enough.

Couples are in a situation where they tend to find themselves in a rocky terrain when the boundary between individual time and joint digital environment may be distorted without clearly understanding the consequences of such a situation, resulting in a situation where one partner feels that he or she is ignored. We can imagine somebody distracted by his or her smartphone over dinner sends the wrong message that he or she is not interested or can be detached, although that is not his or her intention. These situations justify the creation of definite digital boundaries that consider individual and collective requirements.

The best strategy that can be used to define such boundaries is open communication regarding the expectations and levels of comfort that each partner is comfortable with when using the technology. This could come to some terms about where to place certain areas, such as no phone zones or no phone hours, where they could have meaningful time together. An example here would be that couples may conclude that mealtime is a technology-free period that enables them to concentrate only on each other and on the dialogue at the table.

Along with physical boundaries on the usage of devices, it is important to discuss how digital interviews take a toll on the emotional state of individuals. There are a lot of misunderstandings in text-style communications, where tone and context can easily be misplaced. A brief text of only one word Ok may be detected as rude or arrogant, which causes unnecessary tension. In an attempt to counter such miscommunications, couples should embrace the best practices of digital communication by employing emojis or even voice recordings in a bid to express emotion and intent better.

Occasional digital detoxes might help a great deal towards restoring the digital balance in the relationship as well. A weekend away with no screens or a weekly "tech off" night can assist the partners in talking to each other in a less unrealistic manner and on a more responsible level, without all the noise of technology around.

It is also essential that digital boundary violations are approached and worked out of interest rather than judgment. When one of the partners feels ignored because of the phone addiction, talking about it should be more of an open-ended question, not an accusation, since this would lead to a successful conversation. I realized that we had spent time on our phones all night last night. What did you think of that?" Maybe it can be a mild form of initiating the discussion.

After all, drawing digital lines is all about having a certain mindset of understanding and respecting each other's needs and preferences. With the help of developing the digital environment, which focuses attention on the connection and avoids conflict, couples develop resistance to their relations and enhance intimacy in the context of technological challenges of the modern world. This initiative not only reinforces the partnership of the couple but also builds the foundations of a healthier and more communicative relationship, capable of facing the challenges of the digitalized life together.

EFFECTIVE TEXT AND EMAIL COMMUNICATION

The current era is characterized by rapid development and progress of the digital world. Still, text and correspondence over email have become key factors in preserving and developing relationships. Although such communication types are moderately convenient, they harbor special challenges, which may have effects on interrelationships between the partners. The tip in knowing digital communication forms is that of a healthy and positive relationship.

Texting and emailing are, by nature, poor, even more so compared to face-to-face interactions. People can misinterpret and misunderstand due to the lack of voice tone, facial expression, and body language. The text message reply of just a simple ok could be construed as being noncommittal or even rude, depending on what the receiver is in the mood for or is expecting. Though useful, the emojis and GIFs have the potential to mislead the intended emotion or feel of humor. Thus, it is essential to make the digital messages clear and have intentions behind such text.

Couples should leave the notion of clarity and emotional context behind in order to improve communication via texts and emails. This will be possible through the expressive use of language and the integration of digital instruments such as emojis to establish tone and sentiment. It is also possible to add some emotional depth, but voice notes will not. In addition, it can help avoid excessive tension as long as you keep in mind the time and context of messages. The thoughtful message in the middle of the day, like thinking of you, may help to enhance the bonding, whereas a short and abrupt answer during a conflict will fuel the miscommunication.

The third essential facet of digital communication is the creation of limits so that technology can not spoil the relationship but add value to it. Setting up no phone zones at the dinner table or no phone times can also assist in continuing to be present. It is also good that couples talk about what they want in terms of texting frequency and sharing through social media early in the relationship, so conflicts do not arise later.

Couples may want to reconnect digitally and go on a digital detox. Temporary withdrawal from technology contributes to making partners communicate more, become closer, and understand each other. Couples may also use such detoxes to do other activities together, e.g., board games or nature walks, which will further increase the level of communication and minimize distractions on the internet.

In the case of digital miscommunications, it is important to fix them with tact and openness. It is also essential that partners do not hesitate to bring up the time when their signals were misread and ask questions without blaming each other. An innocent question, such as, Did my message come across wrong? It will allow productive discussions and will not allow petty problems to develop.

All in all, effective communication with text and email is aimed at supplementing rather than substituting an in-person conversation. Technology, and digital communication in particular, can be used to strengthen the relationship between couples by pointing out the importance of being intentional with digital messages and setting healthy boundaries. It is also necessary to solve misunderstandings early to prevent them from turning into a conflict. The scenery of the current communication is very complicated. As partners have to live in this situation, the key points are to be attentive and empathetic, and with these characteristics, the relationship can truly have a thriving existence.

NAVIGATING SOCIAL MEDIA

In the real-time world, social media acts both as a connection factor and a disconnection component in relationships in the contemporary world. It is a sphere in which the relationship with others is built with the help of likes, shares, and comments; still, it is a place that can become a root of misunderstandings and misinterpretations. Couples are wading through this terrain by balancing delicate civilizations of the digital-communication world.

The use of social media provides a new method of love demonstration and allows people to stay in contact with each other at any time of the day. A very casual text with the words, e.g., thinking of you, or a common meme, can help strengthen the relationships, showing your love and care in an informal but strong way. Such little actions, if sent digitally, serve as a reminder of existence and attention, making one feel closer when one is apart.

Nevertheless, pitfalls are also possible with the ease of communication through digital means. When the little signs of face-to-face communication are missing, misunderstandings are typical. A text with a full stop may be interpreted as rude, or an emoji may be perceived as sarcastic instead of encouraging. Computer world does not have the color of voice; thus, it mediates possible conflicts based on mere misunderstandings.

In order to curb these problems, married couples should use the best digital communication practices. That involves specific tone and intent, perhaps through the use of voice notes that convey the emotional colour, etc., or as emphasis through the use of emojis in complementing the message. When it comes to digital check-ins, it can also be healthy to set norms so that these interests are not cursory or mechanical but welcoming and encouraging.

In spite of all these initiatives, there will be misunderstandings. When this happens, it is paramount to respond to them directly and with feelings. Easy lines, such as I saw that your response was brief-what happened to be all right? or "Did I sound weird in my text?" may be a gateway towards understanding conversations, where some disagreements are not carried out with significant conflicts.

More than what is being communicated about, other backgrounds, such as how devices are used, count. Tech-related triggers are worth noting, and people should talk to one another about what tech-related behavior is likely to engender disconnection, including checking phones during meals or viewing real-time feeds during intimate moments. To preserve the sanctity of the time, one should create "no-phone zones" or establish a specific time of not being connected so that the partners pay their full attention to each other and are not distracted by digital devices.

Digital detoxes would also be equally crucial at resetting relationships now and then. With a conscious choice to abandon the screens, couples are left to do analog things such as board games, joint cooking, or simply taking a walk. The significance of an even stronger bond that exists beyond the realms of the digital world can also be found in these breaks, as well as the need to remember to be present and attentive.

The most important thing to consider when using social media as a couple is to balance between the online world and the offline world, and that technology is not there to divide but to unite. Couples can improve relationships and take advantage of technological gadgets when they are considerate of how and when they use digital platforms and technologies, which can become a bridge to better comprehension and closeness.

DIGITAL DETOX RITUALS

Technology in a modern relationship is like a two-edged sword. Although it bridges the distance, it also makes invisible partitions in our lives between the two partners occupying the same space. It is common to be physically present with digital devices, which is making them find themselves in a situation where couples are in a form. Yet, they are emotionally disconnected because the screen is dominating their attention, which can be paid to one another. In response to this, it is vital to come up with rituals that will enable couples to disengage with their gadgets and instead spend quality time reconnecting with each other.

The author recommends identifying existing patterns that cause disconnection as the first stage of developing a digital detox ritual. Various couples may not even understand the frequency of time their device cuts into their contact with one another, which can soon turn quality time into a distraction. It could be a common habit, browsing through social media while having dinner, that may make one partner feel overlooked. With such triggers, couples will be able to start establishing realistic boundaries. They could start developing no phone zones during dinners or other more concrete rules that say no devices are allowed in the bedroom after sundown.

When these guidelines are in place, it is possible to bring up the idea of regular digital detoxes as a way of restarting the relationship refreshingly. These clean-outs can be of any size and character, but even temporary breaks will increase the connection to a fine level. As an example, couples can choose to have a so-called Screen-free Saturday morning where they can perform activities that promote intimacy and verbal communication. Going on 'analog date nights' where the couple decides to do something such as board games, walks, or cook together, can be a pleasant break from the digital routine.

Nevertheless, these limits and cleanses are already insufficient solutions. How to go about these digital agreements when they are bound to be violated is also important, as well as strategies. The trick is not to be at fault for such situations but to be curious about them. An example is when a partner accidentally drops his/her phone and goes to it during a no-phone time, the aim should be finding out why it occurred and not being faulty. We can talk softly about how phones interrupted us last night. Has the potential to initiate a discussion that can strengthen the agreement on the digital boundaries without causing further conflict.

Devices are a concern when it comes to developing those digital detox rituals within a relationship; it is not necessarily about being disconnected, but connected to the relationship. The rituals provide the partners with a place where they can interact without being afraid to go away because of notifications and updates. They teach couples to be here, to listen, actually to see each other. They are much more emotionally intimate and can be very easily forgotten in the era of the Internet.

Nevertheless, the point of digital detox rituals is to remind couples about the need to be present with one another. The couple can deepen the level of connection between them, enhance communication, and make lasting memories that are not shrouded in the halo of screens by simply taking active decisions and choosing to disconnect and to make some efforts to do something together that will bring real face-to-face interaction. All these rituals are a reflection of the strength of purposeful interconnection and the brilliant effects it could have on creating successful relationships in a thriving environment.

CHAPTER 10

Healing and Forgiveness

UNDERSTANDING APOLOGY LANGUAGES

Apologies are both a communication act, not just a relationship repair part. Like there is the language of day-to-day communication, there also exists a language of apologies, learning which can completely change how couples interact in conflict and repair emotional barriers. Individuals have different ways of receiving and viewing apologies, and it is therefore necessary that partners regard and react to the distinctions of this process in order to effectively reconcile.

Apology languages propose that the idea of the universality of apology languages is, in most cases, inadequate. The apologies are said to be in five different languages, and people prefer the apologies to be made in different ways. The initial one is saying you are sorry, and this entails no less than a genuine concession to the pain inflicted, typically with words that frankly address the emotional charge on the other person. The literature of "I am sorry the pain I have caused" adds up to the feelings of some who appreciate this type of apology.

The second language is taken responsibility, which is not just any expression of regret but also an acknowledgment of the blame. This is an apology in which there are statements such as: I was wrong, and this is very important to people who require the person on the other end (partner) to own up/their actions. They can be used to rebuild trust and demonstrate that a person is ready to accept their mistakes.

The third apology language is making restitution, and here emphasis is made on making amends. The people who prize this kind of apology will demand that words are not sufficient, and they would like to observe some deeds that could prove the commitment to redress the wrongs. This may include actions taken to address the situation or actions that show goodwill and an intention of fixing it.

Genuinely repenting is the fourth language, which entails the will to change. It is not merely an issue of regretful expression or accountability issues, but of being willing to change. This may involve the pledge to ensure that they do not commit the same mistakes again, and how to curb such problems in the future.

The fifth apology language is asking for forgiveness. To some others, forgiveness necessitates the desire to do so on the part of the one who wronged them in the first place (i.e., the offender). This form of apology initiates a conversation on whether the victim is willing to forgive so that he or she can air his or her sentiments and needs.

Being familiar with these languages helps couples state an apology in the way their spouse likes, and so this would not just be an act of remorse but also effective. It can be advantageous when couples make the effort to explore their respective and each other's apology languages, and this can be done through a quiz or meditative dialogues. Such a realization may avoid misunderstandings and can make apologies, resulting in real healing and reconciliation.

Relationships with differences in apology languages may experience dishonest situations where the tension between the parties is not resolved. Through the sharing and agreeing on the giving and receiving of apologies, couples can close the grey areas that could have caused some conflict that was not mitigated before. This individualization of apologies creates a stronger bond and a stronger relationship, leading towards permanent emotional healing and recovery.

PRACTICING FORGIVENESS

Forgiveness is one powerful thing witnessed in the complex dance of relationships; it is not a means of forgetting past wrong, but rather relinquishing one's hold on the present. There is a common misconception that forgiveness is condoning hurtful behavior or forgetting the pain that was caused. However, sincere forgiveness is when a person is no longer entangled with feelings of resentment and when there is space between healing and growth.

Forgiveness does not happen linearly; it is a process that needs to be pulled away from one. Forgiveness is something that the couples will be advised to embrace with a different kind of understanding that should not involve forgetting the pain, but changing its effects. This change or shift starts by breaking the usual myths and misconceptions about forgiveness, like saying that forgiveness releases the offender or assuming that forgiveness signifies weakness on the side of the forgiving person. Forgiveness, on the contrary, is a healing force that makes people regain their emotional health.

To do this, the couples may participate in specific rituals or visualizations that involve giving up the old pains. These practices also offer a safe environment where they both get a chance to say what each one of them is willing to forgive, and what still has to be processed. By communicating with each other, the partners will express what they feel, and this will lead to common understanding and sympathy.

Establishing clear boundaries is also a part of the forgiveness journey, and once they are in place, they serve as further protection of emotional safety and establishment of simple trust. These lines can be considered new agreements or boundaries that can prevent future hurts and allow both parties to feel respected and valued. By setting such limits, couples are forming a guideline around which they can allow forgiveness to bloom without ending up violating their emotional integrity.

In addition, forgiveness is not limited only to forgiving the partner; it also involves self-forgiveness. In many cases, people set unrealistic standards for themselves, and they judge and feel guilty about such standards. Through the practice of self-forgiveness, one is in a position to shed these self-inflicted burdens and learn to treat oneself with a lot of compassion. Such self-compassion, in turn, supplements the partnership, making the two people develop peacefully.

Rebuilding trust is incorporated into forgiveness in a relationship. Once trust is lost, it is comparable to a bank account that has to be filled in with positive action, together with keeping promises, and so on. Couples are advised to take part in those trust-building actions and rituals that indicate dependability and consideration. This may be as straightforward as regular daily actions or as formal as checking on progress and corrective measures to counteract losses.

By doing this continuous process, the process of forgiveness is made a very dynamic and moving process, and not just a process of healing an old wound, but actually reinforcing the background of the relationship. It is an adherence to expansion, survival, and the collective process of recovery. Forgiveness will enable couples to turn their relationship into an environment of respect, understanding, and everlasting love.

REBUILDING TRUST

It is like trust, once broken, that seems like a thin thread, very fragile, and will be hard to fix. Trust in relationships is not just part of the foundation; it is what binds two people together. This fabric is torn, whether by betrayal, misunderstanding, or neglect, and the effort to mend the fabric seems insurmountable. However, it is not unrealistic. Repairing trust takes effort, time, and the will of both people, and is something that should be done proactively.

The stages start with recognition of the violation. It is vital to appreciate that there is a breach of trust and to realize how much hurt is involved. This recognition does not involve the issue of culpability but rather accepting the reality of the circumstances. Each of the partners needs to realize this by himself or herself and be able to speak openly about this to each other.

Trust will be built through communication. Honest and open communication is the key to making the partners learn the views and feelings of the other partner. This kind of talk must be done with sympathy and a genuine intention to listen. This is important as it will provide an environment where there are no negative expectations, such as judgment. Thus, any partner will feel secure in showing his or her feelings without fear of being punished.

A viable way to regain trust is to establish definite and uniform boundaries. Boundaries can set what is acceptable or not acceptable, and since each partner gets a line on which to operate, there is a way of doing that. Both of them should agree upon these and review them periodically to confirm that they still satisfy the needs of both individuals. Such predictability and openness to a certain amount of consistency in behavior within these boundaries create a sense of reliability and trust, critical constructs.

Besides boundaries, it is possible to create rituals that will be helpful in the trust-building process. These habits, whether it is checking in every day or dating nights once a week, indicate consistent communication and reassurance. They remind me of the dedication every couple has towards the union they are in, and give a chance to celebrate the little wins and successes.

The key role in re-establishing trust is provided by forgiveness. It is a procedure of letting bygones be bygones and deciding to move on. Forgiveness is not forgetting the hurt or forgiving the action that caused the pain. Rather, it is concerned with letting go of the grip the past has on the present so that it opens up to healing and development.

Restoration of trust is also done through action. It takes more than words to say they have to be with reliable behavior. It translates to making good on commitments, responsibility, and reliability. These efforts eventually add up, and they gradually build trust in a relationship.

It should also be noted that there might be a backlash. The rebuilding of trust is not a straightforward process, and episodes of doubt and fear will occur. In such times, open communication is important as well as reinstating the determination towards the restoration of trust. No milestone is too small to celebrate, and it can give the person some sense of motivation and strengthen the progress made.

Eventually, the process of rebuilding trust is concerned with trying to establish a new Chapter of the relationship. It demands investment and commitment of the two parties into the process and in the fact that a better, stronger, and more resilient relationship is achievable. Trust can be restored through patience, effort, and love, and thus provide a stronger and more satisfying relationship.

MOVING PAST RESENTMENT

Even the closest of relationships can be infiltrated with resentment, leeching into the as-yet unnoticed because of the feeling remaining rooted in the other partner. It usually begins with little, unresolved complaints, those little irritants over which one does not even complain; they accumulate like dust in the corners of a relationship. Within the period, these petty frustrations may build up to form a heavy blanket of resentment, which tends to overshadow the intimate relationship between the partners.

Conspiracy of blame is the core of resentment because it is exclusionary and devastating. Most of the time, this cycle starts with unmet needs or unspoken grievances that are turned into grievances when not resolved. Couples can create the effect of seemingly being in the same kind of loop over and over again, recreating what happened previously, and casting it into the present. When this cycle is repeated, it destroys trust and intimacy and creates an environment where the couple members feel that they are opponents instead of allies.

The blame game is very harmful in order to get over resentment, and what couples need to do is abandon this blame game and create an atmosphere where grievances can be aired without the fear of judgment or retribution. This is by creating an atmosphere in which both partners are given a free atmosphere to express their thoughts and frustrations. Structured dialogues where partners agree to engage in listening without interruption and only concentrate on the understanding part and sssnot on the defending side or counterattack are another productive way of achieving this. The practice not only enables the detection of the core reasons behind the resentment but also contributes to the development of empathy and understanding.

The last essential action that leads to getting out of resentment is shifting the blame language to a teamwork language and problem-solving. This transformation includes rephrasing such accusatory phrases as you always or you never with more positive phrases, such as " how can we " and teamwork and support each other. To illustrate, instead of telling a partner that they never get to help around the house, a spouse can tell the partner how they can share their household roles better. This is a minor alteration of the wording, but it sometimes can make a lot of difference and put the conversation in the wrong direction of joint problem-solving, instead of placing the blame.

The check-ups are also important in preventing resentment from taking root. They can be monthly or quarterly ceremonies during which the couples take time to review and sort out any outstanding frustrations or unmet needs. These sessions are meant to air them out so that the partners can disperse any built-up tensions before they harden into resentment. Such rituals as writing letters of resentment release or using a candle, representing the release of the old grudges, may be very potent in such sessions.

In the end, to move beyond resentment, you need to commit to active communication and relationship building. It entails acknowledging and solving minor complaints before they extend further, as well as forgiveness and persistence towards trust-building. In such a way, a couple will be able to turn the resentment into a possibility to become better people, get closer, and become closer to each other.

CHAPTER 11

Future Planning and Goal Setting

VISIONING EXERCISES

In the intricacy of a couple's life, the ability to picture a life together becomes one of the keystones to progress and togetherness. Visioning exercises are a process that engages the partners in thinking outside the box and dreaming up together the roadmap by getting to share the same aspirations and values. Through these exercises, couples will be in a better position to develop a deeper understanding and collective sense of purpose to have a harmonious experience in the relationship.

Under the concept of visioning, the establishment of dreams and goals is advised, where couples do not speak as individuals but as the entire unit. This would be to dwell on the bountiful opportunities that the future has in store, not only in the personal milestones, but also in our mutual life together. The exercise of coming up with a relationship bucket list may be especially enlightening. It enables the partners to brainstorm and list down the things that they want, whether it could be destinations of places in which they want to go, life milestones, personal goals that they want to achieve, or a lifestyle change as a concrete representation of what they want as a product of this vision together.

Another very significant activity that can heighten the congruence between a couple is a shared future letter. Here, they write letters to their future selves (five years later), and each partner does this, pretending what life will look like at that time. This letter is not just wishful thinking, but is more of a story of how they see their lives to be together, along with individual growth being intertwined with shared accomplishments. When the two read these letters to each other, they can be motivated to have meaningful conversations on what is important to them and what needs to be done in order to achieve their dreams together.

Visioning practices also help couples explore the discussions about the changes in their desires and priorities. This is done by saying, with a soft voice, what one partner wants to see more or less of in the relationship, and what new adventures the partner is looking forward to involving the two in. Questions like, What do we want to be in the next season of life in terms of being a couple? Become a spur to these conversations and will encourage partners to reflect and formulate their changing identities and aspirations.

Couples should find the help of frameworks that are able to assist in the determination and monitoring of common objectives to make dreams a reality. Larger ambitions should be dismantled into quicker, achievable actions so that the realisation of the progress does not remain in the field of dreams but a reality that is pursued. One of the most fun ways to think and partake in visualizing these goals and then committing to them is to create a "vision board" collectively. It is a constant reminder of what they want to achieve in life, and it reminds them of their dedication to achieving the same together by always looking at this visual representation.

Further, the critical part is that the couples should not have a vision as a plan but as a living document. The inconsistency of life requires openness and a chance to edit and make adjustments when the times change. Periodic rituals of vision check-ins, which have the effect of reviving and rewriting their goals so that their common vision continues to be inspiring and up to date. The check-ins may align with key moments of a life or be on a semi-annual/annual basis and offer an organized time to have a party on the progress and make adjustments, when necessary.

Finally, dreaming is not the end goal of visioning practices; it is the need to integrate dreams with daily realities so that the dreams will inform the couple how they act and make decisions. In these exercises, couples are able to develop a strong and positive system of relating to each other, a system under which each will be able to grow and, at the same time, achieve a fulfilling relationship.

SETTING SHARED GOALS

The establishment of common goals is one of the fundamentals of building solidarity and a sense of interdependencies in the development of a relationship. The open and honest exchange of dialogue is the starting point to this process, where each partner shares his or her aspirations and desires. In such a dialogue, a couple will be able to find neutral ground, so their goals will be synchronized in order to build a unified perception of the future.

Parallel aspirations are important because they should be used to give direction to a relationship and provide one with purpose. By sitting down and defining their dreams and goals, the partners come up with a roadmap that dictates their moves and decisions. This roadmap is not constrictive since it is a dynamic framework that evolves alongside the maturity of the relationship and changing situations. Periodically revisiting and revising their goals guarantees that the goals are kept current and in line with the changing realities of their lives and aspirations.

One more tool that can be used to improve communication is setting shared goals. The process emboldens the couples to discuss in detail things that really matter to them, building a better comprehension of the value and priorities of one another. It is important in developing a good base of trust because it ensures a partner that the desires and needs are felt and respected.

Further, common ambitions serve as an incentive that pushes couples to strive together in an attempt to realize their goals. Many of these goals involve teamwork and compromise, and these are all important skills in having a healthy and fruitful relationship. They gain a sense of working together as partners, especially when they work towards achieving their mutual goals and commitments, which makes them stronger for each other.

It is not an easy task to set shared goals. It is tolerant and adaptive, and it needs to have the guts to have hard dialogues. There can be differences in the priorities or the approaches, and this has to be negotiated and compromised. Nevertheless, these difficulties can be evolutionary and provide the chance of improvement and strengthening the relationship.

In order to ensure that the establishment of common goals is undertaken, couples may have to participate in a variety of activities that will encourage dialogue and innovation. An example of this is creating vision boards to enable the couple to visually manifest their goals and desires and show how their dreams can overlap. It may also be a lovely practice to write a common packet of their joint futures when couples are asked to describe the vision of their years and plans in a literal form.

And finally, the process of formulating common goals is a process of crafting a common narrative, a story that the partners share and that they both love. This story, then, is a testimony to their life together, a history of their hopes, successes, and loves that hold them together. Accepting shared goals as a practice not only improves the relationship between couples but also lays the foundation for a future full of respect, understanding, and happiness.

TRACKING PROGRESS

Monitoring development in a relationship can be discussed as an important but neglected platform in couple communication. Marking and rewarding small steps toward a better relationship is one way of making a lot of difference in the motivational part of improving. Because the small steps partners take are enough to ignite their motivation, partners can develop a kind of energy that crystallizes the good that they are after in their relationship.

A common practical method that can be used to appreciate improvements would be to celebrate milestones in communications in some creative manner. It can be used to create rituals, rewards, or mini-celebrations when a new habit or breakthrough is attained. As an example, a high-five after a successful check mark or prepping a special dinner in honor of a challenging convo being well managed can be valuable indicators of progress. These are not only the methods of celebration of achievements, but also the construction of a common history of success that can be recalled by partners in rough times.

Another effective way to keep the feeling of victory and persistence in a relationship is to record or publicize victories. Couples can maintain a journal of relationship wins or check with a close friend or therapist who is a witness to the improvement in the relationship. The given practice enables partners to document their achievements and track their progress over time. It is also a chance given to partners to say what they are proud of, and this strengthens their bond to each other and their goals.

Partners may also discuss the status of their achievements after some time, which will help them remember their growth, as well as eventually formulate new micro-objectives. It entails taking stock of what has come before and what has been effective, making a choice on what their intentions will be moving forward as a couple. Examples of questions include: What is one thing we did this month that was better? Or, what new micro-habit do we want to do next? Can we share such thoughts and ensure that the couple remains on the same page about their ambitions?

Effectively, monitoring growth in a relationship has something to do with celebration, documentation, and reflection in a sense. Have small wins, keep records of where you made it, and reflect your progress so the couple can keep the relationship on a positive slope. Such practices can only strengthen the relationship and also create a stronger bond among the partners since they operate together in the realization of their common goal towards tremendous growth and happiness. The phenomenon of monitoring progress changes every single step into a valuable element of the journey of a couple, so that every stage of the development process is recognized and praised.

CELEBRATING ACHIEVEMENTS

Rewarding and honoring even the smallest achievements is a big part of building and fostering relationships. The recognition of even the smallest improvements will then be a strong motivator because it will confirm the direction that a couple is taking towards making positive changes. That is where these small victories offer couples the fuel that they need to continue on their journey together; they will feel motivated and appreciated.

Just think how good it will feel after a whole week with exercises on gratitude every night, when both spouses take a minute to remember how their day was and say what they are grateful for. The ritual changes in tone of appreciation, which go through the relationship, and this increase in intimacy is less emotional than much expected. Every thank you is a rock that leads to a better partnership.

Another creative thing that couples can do is mark the milestones in the way they communicate. These milestones can be something as simple as being able to handle a difficult discussion right or developing a new, healthier habit. No need to make the celebration big, a high-five when checking in successfully or celebrating a special meal after a difficult conversation is managed exceptionally can be extremely meaningful. These are reminders of the accomplishments and power of the bond.

It is also essential to encourage winning couples to record or report their success. Writing a relationship wins journal or bringing progress to a trusted friend or a therapist can give a physical account of progress and improvement. An example would be leaving a voice memo or writing a small win so that you are reminded of the good progress you are making as a team. These records not only show signs of growth but also encourage in times of difficulty.

Another critical factor in terms of celebrating achievements is reflection and mission on growth and establishing new micro-goals. With a retrospective observation of patterns, couples can determine what has yielded positive results and intend to do so in the future. Examples of such questions would be: What is one thing that we improved upon last month? What is one micro-habit that we wish to attempt next month? In so doing, the practice does not discount the accomplishments, but it does provide an active approach to future problems.

After all, relationship milestones and achievements are not merely milestones; they are about the culture of growth and appreciation. It challenges couples not to give up and keeps them working on the better in life without failing to appreciate the efforts and the achievements gained. Attachment to such practices in a relationship helps the couple to develop a sound base of individual respect and admiration, and thus keeps the relationship growing stronger and stronger.

CHAPTER 12

Utilizing Support Networks

BUILDING A SUPPORT ECOSYSTEM

When it comes to communication in a couple, it is essential to create a solid support system that helps them develop a healthy relationship. In addition to the romantic connection between a couple, a sense of deriving strength out of a broader network of relationships that involve friends, family, and mentors, as well as professional resources, needs to be acknowledged. Such an extended network provides a safety net that gives guidance and support, which might enable couples to surpass the trickiness of living together.

The first aspect of developing this support ecosystem consists of finding and nurturing relationships with trusted allies. Partners are advised to create a so-called relationship resource map, a tool that shows the different people and resources that become available to couples. This map is supposed to have friends who are able to give emotional support, family members who are able to give wisdom, and professionals like therapists or coaches who are able to provide some objective support. Seeing these links will help the couples know what they have at their disposal and will be ready to turn to them when a need arises.

It is invaluable to be proactive in dealing with this network. There is no need to come to seek help only when something is going wrong; they should make it their habit to seek help as a preventive measure. Occasional visits from a therapist or mentorship from peers with older couples can ensure that there are proper pieces of advice, and that small troubles do not grow large. The normality of professional and peer solidarity is not only effective in providing relief to the couple but also in establishing a culture of openness and maturity.

Ceremonies are very important in enhancing this support ecosystem. Partners can develop routines of both supporting behaviors and getting supported, and this strengthens their bonds in the network. As an example, one can have a potluck about the topic of relationship wins, establish a night of advice swapping with other couples as a type of community building, and collective learning. These events help them to share experiences, exchange valuable knowledge, celebrate milestones, and meet, thereby making their collective wisdom even wiser.

In addition, it is important to show appreciation to the people who facilitate the relationship. These connections can be fostered through small, thoughtful acts, rather like sending thank you notes to friends or relatives who have specifically assisted or supported. If we make such gestures, we are likely to receive a response, and our swing in each other's direction may increase. Acknowledging the role played by their support network helps the couples value the significance of such relationships and encourages them to continue with mutual support.

Lastly, the establishment of a support ecosystem should be intentional and committed. Couples should be comfortable spending their time and effort in building such links, as they realize that the health of their relationship correlates with that of the community they are in. In such a way, they build a stronger base, covering not only their relationship but enhancing their lives with a variety of opinions and longitudes.

In such a process of an ecosystem of support, couples are given a reminder that they are not on their own. They can always turn to the communal wisdom and power of their people, and they can rely on this communal support at any time they are in need. This expanded network is not a weakness as far as the couple shows commitment to expansion and survivability as it exists to date, in their relationship.

PROFESSIONAL AND PEER SUPPORT

Professional and peer support are two components that cannot be underrated when it comes to relationship development. Couples do need these types of support in order to exist in their complex world of emotions, struggles, and landmarks that define their intertwined world. Professional assistance, which is usually provided through therapy or counseling, gives an organized setting in which couples are encouraged to figure out the dynamics of their relationships with the help of an expert. Invaluable as this professional direction is, it establishes a neutral platform where partners can express their issues and get involved in complicated problem-solving, acquiring new communication skills in the presence of a person who can give objective advice.

A therapist or a counselor is needed to create an understanding and healing so that couples can recognize a pattern that can ruin their relationships. The therapeutic intervention can help the couples have a better understanding of their interactions, learn to offer a better definition of their needs and boundaries, and learn ways of managing conflict through constructive methods. This professional guidance is most needed at a time of transition or a crisis when much depends on it, and feelings run so high. The couple can use a therapist to get to the heart of their relationship with differences by doing this in a safe and encouraging environment. The result can be increased closeness and awareness.

Just as significant is peer support in building relationships. In terms of peer support compared to professional support, the background knowledge of the latter is rather built on the basis of similar experiences and understanding. It entails getting in contact with other couples who are going through the same obstacles, with whom they can share knowledge, support, and camaraderie. Such support is usually informal, conducted through groups like support groups, or in social gatherings where couples are allowed to share their stories and learn how each other coped with the situation.

Peer support is beneficial in many ways. It makes them feel connected with the world and like they belong, which can be immensely helpful to couples who may feel lonely in their plight. Through interacting with their peers, couples get an opportunity to have their same issues looked at through the eyes of people who have no personal interest in the matter and who may be able to offer a different viewpoint and way of handling the situation that they may not have even thought of. Also, peer support might act as a boost of inspiration and motivation since couples see the improvements and strength of the people in similar circumstances around them.

In addition, peer support instills a culture of sympathy and empathy, and couples do not fear expressing their successes and failures because no one would judge. This open discussion is very important in breaking the stigma that accompanies relationship challenges most of the time and helps couples to seek assistance and support instead of struggling alone. Peer support, in this manner, balances professional instruction and offers a holistic approach to relationship development, which also integrates expert advice and community knowledge.

Finally, this integration of professional and peer support will provide a strong support system to the couples, and they will feel strong enough to get through the challenges and grow their bond. They should be able to find solutions to deal with a difficult relationship because they have the resources of their peers and the skills of professionals to help them manage it. Such a double strategy not only has the benefit of improving their interaction and problem-solving capacities but also enriches their heart relationship, which will open the door to a satisfying, successful association.

RITUALS FOR EXTERNAL SUPPORT

External support systems are a big thing, and a lot of the time in the dance of relationships, a lot of things are overlooked. Establishing a strong support network beyond the immediate relationship between the couple can serve as an essential safety net, instill a sense of resistance, and introduce new ways of thinking. Couples that take into account the deliberate development of such networks are usually more skilled at handling the complications of the relationship.

The initial engagement in taking advantage of external support would include appreciating the community. Relationships are not in a vacuum.

They belong to a larger social fabric, which encompasses people and the family, friends, mentors, and peers. Being part of this society can add a lot of knowledge, with wide perspectives and emotional nourishment to a relationship. A small group of couples, a support group, or a couple circle is an example that provides later experiences and common wisdom. It lets the couple connect through group learning and experience.

Designing a support ecosystem for a relationship is a feasible activity that can shed light on available resources for a couple. This entails finding reliable users, who could be friends, relatives, or experts in the field, such as therapists and mentors. Doing a relationship resource map may also be a way of having a visual reminder of these relationship resources. It may be a reminder to the couple to reach out instead of waiting and then reaching out reactively.

The norms of having professional and peer support that keeps a relationship healthy should be accepted. Turning to a therapist or a person who coaches relationships must not be considered a failure, but a good measure towards maintaining growth. On the same note, mentorship by peers, more so older couples who have managed to go through the same situation, may give important input and encouragement.

Rituals are very important in introducing outside support into the life of the couple. Getting a community together is easy; having a potluck party where couples present their relationship victories and strife is a great supportive community event. Likewise, swapping advice nights with other pairs is enlightening, as well as bonding territory that allows one to pick up new strategies and angles.

Another effective ritual that can be used to reinforce some tied external bonds is gratitude. When we send thank you notes to friends or family who have helped us in some way, a thank you note will not only show them appreciation but also strengthen the bonds of the relationship. This act of kindness can turn a network into a support system of individuals and turn it into a cohesive system that will help the couple live a better life.

Drawing someone outside the relationship is a knowledgeable and liberal action. It is about establishing a cadence in which the duo would swing between their intimate world and the larger world and derive energy and influence out of it. Such practices and rituals not only involve seeking help but also paying back; hence, this is the flow of reciprocity of support, which is mutually enriching to the couple and the community.

Eventually, what one hopes to promote is a relationship that is resilient, adaptive, and enriched by the multiple inputs of the surrounding network. The couples will establish a stronger and healthier relationship that is resilient to the changes in life by incorporating external support as a part of the relationship.

SHARING WISDOM AND ADVICE

Wisdom and advice sharing are crucial to creating an enhanced bond when it comes to communication with the couple. It requires both such delicacy as providing insights and maintaining boundaries, as well as the creation of an atmosphere where both partners may feel appreciated and seen. The mentioned practice is not completely about passing pieces of knowledge, but rather having a conversation that would improve understanding and enlightenment within the relationship.

Families find themselves in issues where one of the couples may possess experience or knowledge on a certain matter than the other. In this scenario, the knowledgeable partner should be sensitive and modest during the discussions. This implies the provision of advice that is not taken as a command but as an opinion, giving room to discuss and take a look at the point of view of the second partner. Sentences like, What should we attempt... or "Did you think..." promote a team spirit.

Listening is equally important because it can make a huge difference in the gains and losses that people make when it comes to exchanging advice. Active listening is the main element that makes listening, considering the partner, feeling his/her feelings, and paying attention to them. The practice not only exhibits respect but also creates trust that allows partners to be more open about their thoughts and feelings without the fear of their thoughts being dismissed.

One must also realise when and how to give advice. Giving unsolicited advice, particularly in cases of stress or when one feels weak, may be seen as criticism or even unsupportive. Rather, the couples must endeavor to provide insights to each other in plain, open-door discussions where the involved parties are open. It may include rescheduling a particular time to discuss such topics or having it as part of a routine check-in. Yet, both sides are in a state of mental and emotional readiness to have a constructive dialogue.

The second important thing is the mutual exchange of wisdom. Encouraging either side to contribute their ideas allows equality and instills the fact that both partners can make positive contributions to it. It can be achieved by doing basic exercises such as asking open-ended questions, demonstrating interests in what we think of each other, and consensus retro twinning of what we have experienced. This means that the couples will be able to foster a cozy environment where both partners will feel confident to share and learn with each other.

The manner in which advice is given has a lot to do with the way it is received. Its supportive, non-confrontational warmth will help in the communication of concern and care rather than criticism. Moreover, it is possible to add a touch of humor or something light in order to relieve the tension and avoid making the interaction more formal and serious.

Lastly, it is necessary to keep in mind and notice the effort that both sides of a pair put into giving and seeking advice. Being appreciative of the input and contribution each of the participating individuals brings forth, and with the recognition of the good effects of mutual wisdom, the relationship can be enhanced, and further open communication can be pursued in such a manner. Acknowledging small achievements and thinking about how the piece of advice of the other partner has led to one's own or even to the couple's improvement could still further reinforce the unification of a relationship.

To conclude, it should be said that giving advice and wisdom in the relationship is a process that demands tolerance, understanding, and respect for the other party. This means that, by creating an atmosphere in which both parties feel respected and listened to, couples should be able to employ their shared wisdom and handle the challenges in their lives that will help them to form a more significant and fruitful relationship.

CHAPTER 13

Integrating New Habits

UNDERSTANDING HABIT FORMATION

As to the area of spouses' communication, one should understand the peculiarities of establishing habits. It is the things that we find ourselves doing through the unconscious pressure and automatically develop our relationships, and we call these things habits. They represent the manner of relating to one another and can either make or break the relationship between the partners. The way these habits are formed and modified later is something important to comprehend when it comes to the establishment of the communicative relationship, which is controlled by health.

The psychology of the formation of habit is quite ingrained in the brain, which aims at efficiency. The repetitive action that occurs when the couples react to each other is expounded, and it becomes programmed behavior that does not engage cognitive resources to be used elsewhere. Another source of good that can be introduced in terms of a positive habit is that a person thanks or listens to the other person. However, it is capable of shoving trust and intimacy to the end of developing negative avoidance patterns or criticism sets to the extent of forming them into a habit or pattern.

The couples have to be sensitised to the existing habits that are either negative or positive before any positive changes. All significant change begins here in this consciousness. It is more of setting aside and taking note of what takes place in the relationship on a daily basis. Are you prone to behaving in some particular manner, resulting in a mess or a misunderstanding? Are there rites of passage that create a person-to-person bond and communication? With these patterns, the couples will be able to embark on the understanding of how habits are integrated into their relationship.

Now that awareness is being cultivated, the next step with immediate consequences is to be able to come to a conscious decision of what to change or work on forming habits. This is achieved through the establishment of open intentions and goals of the relationship, bearing in mind the kind of behavior that the parties involved in the relationship like to promote or to get rid of. An example is that two individuals may observe that in the case of an argument, the couple tends to reject the emotions of the other individual and make a determination to listen thoroughly and/or acknowledge the other person. It is a transformation that requires deliberateness on the part of both partners.

A number of strategies are part of the process of habit change. One of the most effective sides of a new habit is habit stacking, which consists of the first habit, bad or good, with the one you want to implement. Using a daily gratitude ritual as an illustration, in the event that a couple wants to use it, they can incorporate it into an existing routine they have, such as sharing a meal. This aids one in memorizing the new habit as it is sponsored by what is familiar.

Accountability is the other critical aspect of developing habits. The second approach to supporting each other is to introduce some check-in calls at particular periods that will discuss the progress and challenges. These are to be done in empathy and predisposition and geared towards applause rather than condemnation. The smallest achievement can also be rewarded, and this will motivate an individual to continue so that he or she can succeed.

Moreover, they should not forget about the rewards of making progress towards creating a habit. One should celebrate small gains as a form of motivation, coupled with reinforcing the targeted behavior. It might be a week of successful communication or even one month without any major argument, but a few minutes to make it a celebration may fortify the relationship and encourage more to do it.

In summary, the idea of habits and the possibility of shaping them can be considered a powerful means of communication. In order to enhance their relationship, couples may establish favorable habits since they will be aware of the existing tendencies, as they have certain goals pre-established, and they support each other throughout the process. The habit forming is an ongoing process and continuing on the process and continuing with one another is the way you can make it through to another much closer state.

DESIGNING NEW RITUALS

Development in relationships based on ritual has been the pillar of relationships and formation. The rituals may turn out to be a fertile theory of enhancing relationships between couples and making the other important, all through attentive and mindful planning and implementation.

Unlike routine, rituals are crammed with purpose and meaning, and this provides couples with the guideline to relate to each other at a dignified level.

The most important principle of the establishment of new rites is that these are not just purposeful but are really adapting and accommodating them to the peculiarities of this or that relationship. All that begins with the questioning of what can be done in the relationship to have a more purposeful interaction. This may include after-work bonding sessions, ways of celebrating successes, and ways of surviving the bad times.

The first step in creating a new ritual involves coming up with an understanding of the components of the relationship, in that an individual would like some form of support or celebration. Human beings can start by thinking of their normal day and observe what appears to be in a hurry or left behind. Perhaps there might be some aspect of the day where we might have a time of gratitude, and the gratitude would be heightened, or there might be a situation where a little but shared inside activity would be very advantageous in building up closeness.

Once such moments are identified, the next step comes when one should brainstorm activities or gestures that one can perform and which both partners are going to love. The disadvantage is that you have to choose things that you can experience as genuine and as positive, not something that is boring or that you have to do. Such a daily routine can be as simple as meeting for morning coffee, where no form of digital intrusion is possible, and it can offer a seamless entry into the day. On other occasions, couples can also determine how they will end their day by telling each other what they liked about the other, and this will provide a culture of appreciation and reward.

Rituals should have a flexible design. The witness may even have altered the character of such practices under the alteration of circumstances.

Partners ought to check their practices constantly; this way, they cannot become a routine or grueling process, and both become noble and lovable. Such malleability avoids the problem of drifting, and ritual continues to live and be relevant.

In addition to the rituals that happen every day, couples may consider some seasonal or annual rituals as well. These are the rituals that mark the huge milestones or life transitions. These can be as casual as annual traveling to reflect on the past year and hear plans on what to expect out of the new year, and even creating an event when we remind ourselves of the achievements we have made in terms of a fancy dinner.

What it implies is that the meaning of a successful ritual is whether the ritual is capable of bringing the partners closer and can provide them a shared experience, which can also contribute to the enhancement of a relationship. When putting time and energy into the business of creating such rituals, a couple is not creating a new appointment in the home calendar; a tapestry of memories is created, which can be utilized in the business of bond strength cementing.

With the help of controlling and elaborating rituals, couples can foster an environment whereby the climate of the relationship is dynamic rather than stable, and relationships can be rendered powerful. The practices may offer a platform where life can be sprinkled with a sense of connection and enjoyment as a way of creating a reminder of the dedication and love that are synonymous with their relationship. This is another way how rituals may not be just a routine, but the heartbeat of a freshly blossomed relationship that makes them endure good times and bad times together.

SUSTAINING LONG-TERM CHANGE

Within the framework of couple communication, the essence of bringing long-term change to life is kept in the fact that the possibility to create gradual development and encourage minor achievements is obtained. Coming to the side of giving rewards and recognition, it is also very important to give a reward for every step that results in heading the right direction, as this not only acts as a motivator but also makes positive changes at the relationship level. An example could be couples having the pleasure of small rituals, such as the appreciation of a week of successful nightly implementation of gratitude, which could act as an incentive to sustain growth.

You should be creative if you wish to celebrate the communication milestones. Couples can establish rituals or rewards, or even a mini-celebration of a newly formed habit or breakthrough. Good top-level reinforcements include a high-five after a session where a lot was accomplished or dinner planned to celebrate a challenging conversation that was discussed professionally. Such rituals constitute the key symbolism of indicating the meaning of intentionality in maintaining change.

Moreover, standardization and printing of triumphs can be of great assistance along the path of improvement. Relationship victories that are recorded in the diary or the other person being brought up to speed and honestly having them see through progress can provide a feeling of accountability and positive reinforcement. The tradition puts into balance the accomplishments and serves as an icon of resilience and tenacity in a pair that is working things out in tandem.

The other defining component is thinking about progress and setting new micro-goals. Afterwards, couples become deliberate about the subsequent steps in the relationship by thinking and arriving at what has worked previously and how this can be implemented in the subsequent steps.

Questions that you might ask yourself are, what is one thing that we did better last month? Or what is the next micro-habit that we want to do? It can guide couples when they act on their ongoing growth and attachment.

Because communication is likely to be the most important factor in keeping the relationship going, it follows that it is necessary to use different methods at the different levels and stages of the relationship. First relationships are both good and harmful to new couples. The initial phase of what others refer to as the honeymoon phase can lay down the seaboard, whether bad or good, in the long term. The inability to participate in hard conversations, being overly accommodating, or romanticizing can backfire in later problems. It is therefore necessary to establish certain ground frameworks in order to establish trust and openness in the beginning. Among the things done so as to establish a foundation to foster open and vulnerable communication are the use of communication checklists within the first year or even sharing future dreams, as part of a weekly ritual.

Long-term relationships may result in plenty of hazards in communications by making use of autopilot or gradual separation due to the absence of being emotional within the communication with each other. Life transformations such as career change, moving home because of a child's birth, or nursing the sick parents can change the pattern in a relationship. To overcome these problems, a couple can re-stimulate their sense of curiosity and emotional closeness to one another with the help of rituals and questions that suggest that they rediscover themselves. Going back to old wounds and renegotiating agreements, long-held relationships would have guidelines such as a 20 Questions exercise with Long-Term Couples or a state-of-us meeting once a month.

Long-term couples need to have an element of marking milestones and development, too. It may be a milestone event, a time to overcome a challenge, creating new promises towards each other. Still, such moments of recognition can provide them with the motivation to persist in being committed, as they must also be emotionally related. Planning out an "accomplishments timeline" or putting a ritual in place for these relationship birthdays can become one of the ways that the couple remembers the past and dreams about the future based upon a hopeful outlook and determination.

CELEBRATING CONSISTENCY

Valuing and embracing the little triumphs of the relationship is a major culture that brings life into a partnership and makes a partnership alive. Each of those steps, no matter how minuscule they may seem to each of the other ones, is a part of the larger piecework of evolution and enlightenment between spouses. The kind of fun in such minor achievements is the mode through which one is enabled to develop motivation and the urge to continue with the line of positive development that is set by counterparts.

Think of the power associated with acknowledging a week of nightly token of gratitude exclamations. When religiously done, such a ritual also becomes a difference maker in the emotional landscape of a relationship because such a routine appears so easy each time you turn it on. This is an expression of the positive encouragement of the concept of appreciation and mindful relationships between the partners, which adds to a good ripple of connectedness. Such recognition instances do not just remain as part of the act but also volunteer the intention to raise and value the relationship.

There are possible ways through which parties can be reached when reaching communication milestones. It could be a high-five when one checks in successfully, or a cook-up to commemorate a tricky talk that was had properly, but in any case, such gestures induce a sense of achievement or even companionship. They are the rituals that signify the strides that have been made in solidifying the commitment of the partners to proceed with their growth endeavors.

Another concept to employ in order to solidify these positive experiences is to put them in a written form and share them. One example is a relationship win journal where couples will have to delve into thoughts of what their experience was and how much they have achieved. Such achievements can even be enhanced by discussing with a close friend or a therapist who would view such achievements as motivation and offer that kind of support.

One should also think of progress and propose some new micro-goals. They can see trends of success and what must be done, and it is these trends that partners can use in order to sketch out where they need to focus. It is a reflection that helps to set some goals for how to improve in the future and keep the growth trend alive. The map of the future growth is assisted with questions like What is one thing that we did better this month. Or what other micro-habit would we like to do?

Such little successes, when done frequently, instill a spirit of gratitude into such a relationship. It also focuses on the importance of the contribution of both partners and making them committed to the group and the specific mission. This field would also be a first in the relationship, a reminder that nothing is bigger than perseverance and commitment.

In essence, rewarding progress is not the only way to be consistent. It means the establishment of an environment of effective and receptive relations where growth is not only anticipated but fostered. It is a matter of establishing a bond that operates on the principle of support and appreciation, and how every step one takes is an opportunity to celebrate and a foundation toward greater heights.

CHAPTER 14

Reflecting and Growing Together

MAPPING COMMUNICATION GROWTH

Growth in couple communication is paramount in defining and charting growth in the establishment of a sound and lasting relationship. The means through which spouses talk to one another, adjust to new realities, and encourage each other should also change along with the relationship. This process starts with self-examination and a commitment that both individuals need to give the relationship itself the time, energy, and care necessary to keep it growing strong.

The first step in communication growth mapping is to be able to perceive the current patterns in the relationship. Couples are advised to study their communication patterns, and these include those that are positive and those that require enhancement. This self-analysis gives an initial idea of how the relationship is faring and some of the potential changes that can be made to do better in terms of mutual understanding and satisfaction.

This can be efficiently done by creating a written or a graphical map of communication. It is considered a diagnostic and roadmap in the sense that such a map would allow partners an opportunity to see their communication terrain. It involves finding out the essential communication requirements, dominant performance points and pitfalls of possible danger points that might result in miscommunication or even demands. By spelling out these factors, couples can come up with mechanisms for dealing with their interactions in a better way.

The map is also expected to identify the triggers that tend to cause conflict and the strategies for resetting what has worked in the yesteryears. This could entail enlisting the most typical sources of conflicts and coming up with solutions to handle them before they snowball into larger areas of disputes. Partners can, in this case, agree on certain phrases or behaviors that would indicate that one or the other needs a break or a change in tone in the conversation.

It is important to review and revise such a communication map regularly as a relationship goes on. Relationships can be affected heavily by factors like a change in career, the birth of a child, or relocation to a new city. With the help of routine check-ins and updates, the couples will have an opportunity to make sure that their communication strategies stay relevant and effective.

The map of the communication should also be visible and accessible. Be it a digital document on a shared folder or a physical map on a common space, leaving this tool in a place where it can be seen and easily accessed helps keep this tool in mind at all times and helps remind the couple every time of their commitment to grow.

Couples are also invited to experiment with new communication rituals that would support and maintain positive communication that has been going on in the past and present. These rituals could be sharing gratitude on a daily or weekly basis, weekly check-ins, or Monthly relationship reviews. These practices not only enrich communication but also increase the level of emotional intimacy and trust.

This process of mapping ensures that, by agreeing to it, the couple gives itself the chance to work through the intrigues of the relationship with more clarity and confidence. It converts the reactive conflict-based process called communication into a proactive growth experience. As the partners collaborate in learning and helping each other meet their needs in a variety of ways of communicating, they set the stage to have a strong and satisfying partnership that can survive and flourish through changes in life.

PERIODIC REFLECTION

Within the context of growing relationships, it is largely left unrecognized, but taking a step back to analyze and feel good about the results is what makes revolutions. Regular reflection is an important resource that can help couples, and it provides a framework during which to stop, reflect, and establish the context of how to proceed going forward. This reflective practice is not just a practice of reporting what has happened. Still, it is a means to discern how the relationship shifts and develops, what needs improvement, and what needs to be celebrated, whether the improvements are big or small.

It starts by making a specific place and time for someone to reflect. Couples should set a habit out of this, and it may be a monthly sit-down or quarterly getaway. The trick is consistency and purpose, and in this way, both parties can afford to use an open and candid conversation that will be as honest as it will be hopeful. In these sessions, partners will be able to look at myriad tools to enable this reflection. Depending on their uniqueness, these tools may be as simple as a mood chart or a more technical progress tracker, which illustrates in visual form the journey they have begun going through together.

One of the most vital elements of periodic reflection is what is referred to as relationship wins. These are all the milestones that usually pass unnoticed in the workaday bustle. When a couple records and celebrates these instances, they make the positive behaviors stronger, in addition to creating a pool of joint accomplishment and happiness. The practice can be used to create a culture of gratitude and positive attitude culture, which is a cushion against the unavoidable problems that will come in any relationship.

In addition to this, a periodical reflection motivates one to plan future objectives. Such a future-oriented nature is what turns the reflection operation into an active developmental plan. This will be the time that couples can sit down and come up with new connection goals, in which they see the future of their connection in terms of the next step. Intensifying communication, discovering new things in common, or increasing emotional integration these are some of the objectives that give the relationship future directions.

To facilitate this, couples may use multiple templates and worksheets that would help them to have the conversation. An example of this would be the creation of a growth map worksheet, to give partners an idea of the journey they have previously taken and where they want to head towards, whilst a before-and-after communication self-assessment could inform them of what they have managed to fix, which needs to be addressed. Not only do such tools make the abstract nature of growth and change concrete, but they also establish in it a feeling of responsibility and investment in the evolution of the relationship.

Also, the benefits of being able to reflect periodically can be increased when these insights and achievements are shared with a broader support network, say a therapist or a couples group. This social component not only gives them external confirmation but also brings a variety of voices and opinions that can make the path of the two more productive.

Periodic reflection is, at its essence, about writing a story of developing, fighting hardship, and helping each other to achieve. It is about understanding that the relationships are not constricted but dynamic things that blossom with attention and care. Through the process of regularly taking time to engage in this reflective practice, couples will be able to build the type of relationship that is robust, robust enough to withstand the storms and rejoice in the sunshine. Such a continuous conversation helps not only to make the relationship between the partners stronger but also to make a better understanding and appreciation in the joint path of love and companionship.

ADAPTING TO LIFE CHANGES

Life is a woven tapestry of experiences, and in many instances, couples have to jump through hoops in order to cope with the changes that may transform the entire topography of their relationships. Both expected and unexpected changes come along with their sentiments, where flexibility and understanding are required. Couples stand to transition either through their careers, birth of children, or other changes that their age could bring on; adaptability is therefore paramount. It is here that communicative action comes into focus in the sense that it is a connecting ingredient and a guide to the shifting landscape of living together.

Any change involves the acceptance of change as inevitable. The couples need to understand that change should not be considered as interference but rather as a progression of their common journey. This attitude change enables partners to have an inquisitive attitude to transitions instead of resistance. Accepting a change as an opportunity to grow, couples will ensure a positive outlook that will make them resilient and open-minded.

The second successful action plan that can be recommended in changing situations is to create some new communication rituals. These rituals can be as minimal as reserving time to communicate once a week or to maintain a joint diary where both sides can write whatever they feel and what they are concerned about. Such practices promote the continuation of conversations and offer a platform to speak about the influence of life changes on the relationship so that couples can solve problems before they become ones and find better ways to respond to problems than react to them.

The other important ingredient in being able to adjust to changes in life is flexibility. When the relationships within the relationship are changed, the partners might have to negotiate on roles and expectations. This involves the ability to re-open and rewrite contracts so that they are up to date and suit the needs of both parties. Discussions in these adjustments will help one avoid misunderstandings, a sense of being complementary and collaborative.

Support is essential when change takes place. Couples must invest in developing such a secure environment where the partners can expect to be listened to and understood. This means listening actively and empathizing with each partner as it is through this way that a partner is free to state his/her fears and desires without any form of judgement. Couples need higher trust and emotional safety that will help them relax and go through the changes more easily.

Also, praising small milestones and victories would help strengthen positive adaptation. It can be the positive impact of recognizing the good way one has dealt with a stressful situation, or just the act of appreciating each other, whether it is hard work or otherwise, such celebrations can support one another in their feelings of appreciation and dedication towards each other. These Cuban gestures are used to remind them of the strength of the couple and how they can survive the change.

Flexibility, communication, and provision of emotional support become part of life, which not only allows couples to become accustomed to changes, but also to develop through them. Viewing change as the natural occurrence of their life experience, couples will be able to turn various difficulties into possibilities of strengthening their link and enhancing their perception. This way, adjusting to the new life is no longer a consuming challenge that requires one to figure out solutions, but accepting the challenges to live with assurance and a sense of togetherness.

INSPIRING LASTING CONNECTION

When relating to another person, creating a meaningful, long-term relationship is both something that takes work, effort, and practice. At the core of this effort, emotional intimacy cultivation is the key to a strong partnership. There is also encouragement for the couples to develop some habits where they get to understand each other deeply, thus building a relationship that does not waver with time.

Open communication is one of the key factors in the development of a long-term relationship. This is not something one shares their thoughts and feelings, and it involves active and empathetic listening. When listening empathetically, the couples will overcome the superficial level of interaction and be able to enter the inner circles of their experiences. Such communication is not about resolving the others' issues but simply being there and acknowledging the feelings of the others.

The other effective tool is the development of common rituals to help build stronger bonds. Such rituals may be as basic as daily meetings or as formal as monthly state-of-the-union meetings. These kinds of practices are systematic moments that help partners review their relationship, enjoy some milestones, and have some new objectives to accomplish together. Through embedding these rituals, couples can give their relationship a sort of continuity and progress, which in turn would strengthen their commitment to one another.

Spontaneity is more to the relationship being alive, on top of structured communication. The spark can be rekindled by introducing aspects of surprise and novelty, in the form of doing something new with them, or making unexpected plans together. This combination of predictability and zest will allow finding the middle ground between stability and thrill, and make it possible to be excited and satisfied with the relationship on a long-term basis.

This is yet another path through which long-lasting bonds are developed by exploring life together. It does not matter whether they need to handle career change, family relations, or self-development, as a couple, they will be able to overcome any obstacle and become stronger and closer to each other. This means helping one another through transitioning, encouraging one another, and being flexible with the changing circumstances. Couples can strengthen their bond and develop resilience by considering a challenge as a way of growing instead of a hindrance.

Moreover, it is essential to stress the role of forgiveness and releasing past grievances. Resentment is something that can destroy the basis of any relationship. Rather, the couples are advised to learn how to forgive and forget the grip of previous wounds, and to move on with the present and future. This process can be done by having open conversations on what is not going right and a possible agreement to start again with a new sense of trust and feeling.

The bottom line of inducing an enduring relationship is the provision of a relationship ambiance in which both partners feel appreciated, understood, and liked. It is about creating a lasting partnership, not only to last but also to succeed; one that grows with time and nourishes as it grows with each other's experience and development. With the adoption of these principles, couples will have a form of relationship that is not only sustainable but extremely fulfilling and that serves as a source of love and companionship in any given relationship, which enhances life.